Syrian Notebooks

Syrian Notebooks

Inside the Homs Uprising
January 16–February 2, 2012

Jonathan Littell

Translated by Charlotte Mandell

VERSO
London • New York

Supported using public funding by

ARTS COUNCIL
ENGLAND

This book has been selected to receive financial assistance from English PEN's "PEN Translates!" program, supported by Arts Council England. English PEN exists to promote literature and our understanding of it, to uphold writers' freedoms around the world, to campaign against the persecution and imprisonment of writers for stating their views, and to promote the friendly cooperation of writers and the free exchange of ideas. www.englishpen.org

First published in English by Verso 2015
Translation © Charlotte Mandell 2015
Introduction © Jonathan Littell 2015
First published as *Carnet de Homs: 16 janvier–2 février 2012*
© Gallimard 2012

1 3 5 7 9 10 8 6 4 2

Verso
UK: 6 Meard Street, London W1F 0EG
US: 20 Jay Street, Suite 1010, Brooklyn, NY 11201
www.versobooks.com

Verso is the imprint of New Left Books

ISBN-13: 978-1-78168-824-3
eISBN-13: 978-1-78168-826-7 (US)
eISBN-13: 978-1-78168-825-0 (UK)

British Library Cataloguing in Publication Data
A catalogue record for this book is available from the British Library

Library of Congress Cataloging-in-Publication Data

Littell, Jonathan, 1967–
[Carnets de Homs. Engish]
Syrian notebooks / Jonathan Littell.
pages cm
Translation of: Carnets de Homs : 16 janvier–2 février 2012; first published: Paris : Gallimard, 2012.
ISBN 978-1-78168-824-3 (hardback : alkaline paper)
1. Syria—History, Military—21st century. 2. Revolutions—Syria—History—21st century. 3. Civil war—Syria—History—21st century. 4. Homs (Syria)—History, Military—21st century. 5. Homs (Syria)—Social conditions—21st century. 6. War and society—Syria—Homs—History—21st century. 7. Littell, Jonathan, 1967– –Travel—Syria. 8. Foreign correspondents—Syria—Biography. I. Title.
DS98.6.L5713 2015
355.009569104'2—dc23
2014048357

Typeset in Monotype Fournier by Hewer Text UK Ltd, Edinburgh, Scotland
Printed in the US by Maple Press

Table of Contents

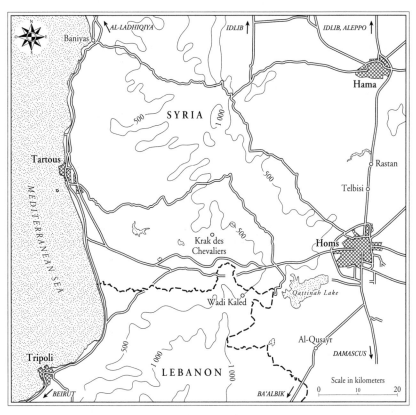

Homs and the Border Region

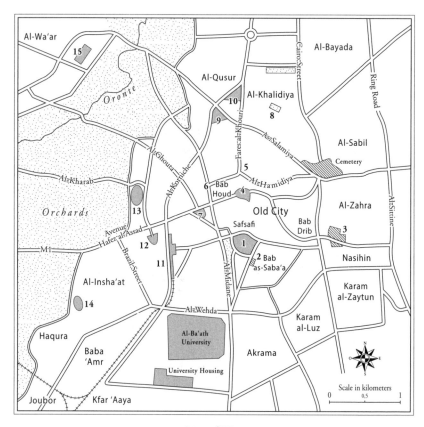

City of Homs

1- Citadel of Homs
2- Bab as-Saba'a Cemetery
3- Bab Drib Cemetery
4- Souk
5- Old Clock Tower
6- City Center (New Clock Tower)
7- Mosque Ad Droubi
8- Square of Free Men (Al-Khalidiya)

9- National Hospital
10- Bus Station
11- Homs Station
12- Safir Hotel
13- Khalid ibn Walid
14- Al-Bassel Stadium
15- Military Hospital

Introduction to the Verso Edition

The world is not yours alone
There is a place for all of us
You don't have the right to own it all.

— An anonymous Syrian yelling in the night
at a regime sniper, in footage included
in the film *Silvered Water*

It starts, as always, with a dream, a dream of youth, liberty, and collective joy; and it ends, as all too often, in a nightmare. The nightmare still goes on and will last much longer than the dream: struggle as they can, no one knows how to wake up from it. And it keeps spilling over, infecting ever wider zones, all the while seeping through our screens to come lap up against our gray mornings, tingeing them with a distant bitterness we do our best to ignore. A vague and remote nightmare, highly cinematographic, a kaleidoscope of mass executions, orange jumpsuits, and severed heads, triumphant columns of looted American armor, beards and black masks, and a black banner all too reminiscent of the

pirate flags of our childhoods. Spectacular images that have
served to mask, even erase, those forming the undertow of
the same nightmare: thousands of naked bodies tortured
and meticulously recorded by an obscenely precise administration, barrels of explosives tossed at random on
neighborhoods full of women and children, toxic gasses
sending hundreds into foaming convulsions, flags, parades,
posters, a tall smiling ophthalmologist and his triumphant
"re-election." The medieval barbarians on one side, the
pitiless dictator on the other, the only two images we retain
of a reality far more complex, opposing them when in fact
they are but two sides of the same coin, one coin among
many in a variety of currencies for which no exchange rate
was ever set.

The notes that form this book are a record of a brief
fragment of the dream: a dream that was already assailed on
all sides and subjected, as we will see, to unutterable
violence, but one that the dreamers still clung to, with all
their heart and all their strength. Publishing them now,
reopening this small window on three weeks lost in the
distant past – three years ago, an eternity – may at least
serve this purpose: to remind the reader that before the
nightmare, a nightmare so dense and opaque it seems to
have no beginning, there had been the dream. And that
whereas nightmares are a roiling magma of individual
pulsions, deriving their shape only from the hollow molds
of ideology, and adding up to nothing but death, dreams
are collective, political, spiritual, social. Perhaps then, these
notes might help provide a touchstone, a reference point,
to show that all this did not happen by chance; more

importantly, that all this did not have to be, that there were other paths, other possibilities, other futures. That the mantra so tirelessly repeated by our solemn leaders, "There is nothing we could have done," is simply not true. And that without our callous indifference, cowardice, and short-sightedness, things might have been different.

When the photographer Mani and I arrived in Homs, in mid-January 2012, the Syrian revolution was reaching the end of its first year. In the city and the surrounding towns, the people were still gathering daily to demonstrate – calling for the fall of the regime, loudly asserting their belief in democracy, in justice, and in a tolerant, open, multi-confessional society, and clamoring for help from outside, for a NATO intervention, for a no-fly zone to stop the aerial bombardments. The Free Syrian Army (FSA), made up mostly of Army and secret services deserters disgusted by the repression, still believed its primary mission was defensive, to protect the opposition neighborhoods and the demonstrations from the regime snipers and the feared *shabbiha* (mafia thugs, mainly Alawite in Homs, formed into militias at the service of the al-Assad family). The Syrian citizen-journalists, like those that helped, guided, and protected us during our stay, still believed that the constant flow of atrocity videos they risked their lives every day to film and upload on YouTube would change the course of things, would shock Western consciousnesses and precipitate strong action against the regime. The people still believed that song, dance, slogans, and prayer were stronger than fear and bullets. They were wrong, of course, and their illusions would soon drown in a river of blood.

America, traumatized by two useless and disastrous wars to the point of forgetting its own founding myth – that of a people rising against tyranny with their hunting guns, helped only by indomitable spirit and idealism – stood back and watched, petrified. Europe, weakened by economic crisis and self-doubt, followed suit, while the regime's friends, Russia and Iran, occupied every inch of the political space thus made available. And geopolitics is always written with the blood of the people. The day after I left Homs, on February 3, a series of mortar shells targeted the neighborhood of al-Khalidiya, where I had spent so much time, killing over 140 civilians. As Talal Derki, the Syrian director and narrator of the magnificent documentary *Return to Homs*, comments at that point in his film, this mass murder was the turn of the revolution: "The dream of a revolution with songs and peaceful protests ended."

I have already described, in the epilogue I wrote a few months after my stay in Homs, the events that followed: the Army's total destruction and occupation of the "free neighborhood" of Baba 'Amr, and the beginning of the bitter siege of the opposition neighborhoods in the center. This siege, which leveled large parts of the city, lasted over two years: finally, in May 2014, the exhausted and starved survivors brokered a deal, and were allowed to evacuate the city alive, abandoning the empty ruins to the triumphant regime. This event was hardly noticed in the West; others were captivating our attention. Just as we only woke up to the threat of Ebola when the first cases hit Texas and Madrid, shrugging helplessly and even indifferently as long as it was only killing Africans, so did we only finally react to the horror engulfing Syria and then Iraq when images of Western journalists and aid workers, kneeling in orange jumpsuits to have their heads sawed off by some masked British psychopath, were forcefully shoved down our throats, in all the perfection of their sickening *mise-en-scène*. A year earlier, on August 21, 2013, the Syrian government had shelled rebel Ghouta suburbs of Damascus using sarin, a lethal nerve agent, killing hundreds, perhaps even more than a thousand civilians and blatantly violating every single "red line" set by Western democracies. France (who to its credit always seems to have had a more lucid vision than its partners regarding the perils of an extension of the conflict), was prepared to join an international coalition and engage in punitive airstrikes against key regime bases and facilities, but was forced to stand down when first the UK and then the US, for mostly internal political reasons, backed off and brokered a vague chemical disarmament deal with Russia, granting the regime a new lease of life as the only power in the region technically capable of carrying out such a disarmament, and in the process permitting it to continue mass-murdering its civilians using more conventional weaponry, such as Scud rockets, artillery, and barrels crammed with explosives. Meanwhile, more and more voices were rising, in the West and elsewhere, to suggest that the real peril was not al-Assad and his oppressive regime, but the growing Islamist threat, most violently incarnated by the self-proclaimed "Islamic State in Iraq and Syria," Da'esh in its Arabic acronym.

Mani and myself happened to be in Homs, and were able to document what seems to have been the first deliberate sectarian massacre of the conflict, the murder with guns and knives of an entire Sunni family in the Nasihin neighborhood on the afternoon of January 26, 2012.[1] Many more would follow, first of other families, then of entire Sunni communities in the village belt surrounding Homs to the West, in the foothills of the Jabal an-Nusayriyah, the so-called "Alawite mountain" from which the regime continues to draw its main support. Up to that point, as all our interlocutors kept repeating to us and as we witnessed in the demonstrations, the revolutionaries were doing everything in their power to prevent the descent into sectarian warfare; the FSA response to this massacre was not to slaughter an Alawite family, but to attack the Army checkpoints from which the murderers had come. Yet provoking widespread ethnic and sectarian conflict was clearly becoming one of the main regime strategies. It made a perverse kind of sense. Even though the al-Assad power structure was founded not, as is often said, on an exclusively Alawite basis, but on an alliance between the Alawite ruling clique and a Sunni bourgeoisie – already established or newly promoted and granted key posts in the economy, the bureaucracy, and even the Army and security services – the regime felt it could no longer trust the Sunni, and banked its survival on the mass mobilization, in its favor, of the country's numerous small minorities: not just the Alawites but also the Ismaelites and the Christians, as well as the Druze and the Kurds if possible. Not even all the Alawites, at the beginning, fully supported the regime; the Christians, as can be seen in this book, were often neutral, as were other minorities. And after being forced to purge most of its

---

1   See the corresponding chapter in this book.

unreliable Sunni troops, to the point of disarming entire divisions, the Army desperately needed fresh recruits. The opposition sought to resist these sordid provocations as best it could, but in vain. By mid-2012, uncontrolled FSA elements were also carrying out sectarian massacres in Alawite villages, and the downward spiral accelerated dramatically. Most minorities, whether they wanted to or not, found themselves taken hostage by the regime: the Kurds brokered their tacit support in exchange for near-total political autonomy; as for the Alawites, hesitant or not, the cycle of massacre and counter-massacre turned the regime's survival into an existential question for them, making the entire community into accomplices.

But transforming a popular, broad-based, proletarian and peasant uprising into a sectarian civil war was not the regime's only card. From the very beginning, the Damascus propaganda machine had sought to paint the revolutionaries as terrorists and Islamist fanatics. What was missing were the real ones; but the regime would do everything in its power to draw them into the game. As soon as the uprising gained momentum, in the spring of 2011, the *mukhabarat*, Syria's feared secret services, released scores of jihadist cadres detained in their jails. And there is much anecdotal evidence that they favored the rise, throughout 2012, of the radical Islamist armed groups that would soon enter into conflict with the more secular FSA. When Da'esh first began conquering territory in Syria, in January 2013, "they never fought the Damascus regime and only sought to extend their power over the territory freed by our units," as an FSA fighter, the son of a landowner from the powerful Syrian al-Jabour tribe, explained in September 2014 to a journalist from *Le Monde*. "Before their arrival, we were bombed each day by the Syrian air force. After they took control of the region, the bombing immediately stopped." Little wonder that in spite of their very un-Islamic reign of terror many civilians living under Da'esh control, in towns such as ar-Raqqah, now feel "safer" there than in other parts of Syria. And when in December 2013 the FSA, newly allied with other Islamist rebel groups such as the Al-Qa'ida spin-off Jabhat al-Nusra, finally launched an offensive against Da'esh, triggering a new and ultra-violent "war within the war," the regime artillery and air force continued bombing only the anti-Da'esh forces, sparing once again the troops of the "Islamic State." It is facts such as these that finally led French Foreign Minister Laurent Fabius to publicly denounce, in the summer of 2014, the "objective complicity" between Damascus and Da'esh. Yet no matter how cynical, none of this is very surprising. As *Le Monde*'s Christophe Ayad wrote in a May 2014 portrait of the leader of Da'esh, Abu Bakr al-Baghdadi:

> The Syrian secret services, who have spent most of their time since 2003 managing, infiltrating, and exfil-trating jihadists transiting to Iraq [to fight US forces], know their "clients" very well, when they are not directly manipulating them. They know that the first objective of most of them is the creation of a Caliphate strictly applying sharia law, rather than the promotion of democracy in the Middle East.

Playing the extremists against the moderates – the basic idea being that, having little or no social base, radical forces will be easy to eliminate once they have helped with the far harder job of crushing a main opponent deeply rooted in society — is a strategy that certainly has its *lettres de noblesse*. Practiced ineptly, as it usually is, it has an unfortunate tendency to turn against its initiators, as in the case of Israel when it quietly fostered the rise of Hamas in the hope of bringing down Arafat's PLO, or the United States when it armed the more radical jihadists against the Soviets in Afghanistan, sealing the doom of the moderate mujahideen factions and unleashing forces still not contained to this day. But on occasions it can bring a measure of success, at least in the short term. Chechnya is a case in point. After Russia's humiliating defeat there, in August 1996, at the hands of a few thousand rebels armed only with Kalashnikovs and RPGs, the Russian special services, FSB (the successor organization to the KGB) and GRU (military intelligence), immediately began preparing the grounds for the next conflict. The three years during which a de facto independent Chechnya managed its own affairs rapidly turned into a disaster: the systematic kidnappings of foreign journalists and aid workers, culminating in the spectacular decapitation of four British and New Zealander telecom engineers in December 1998 by the well-known Islamist commander Arbi Barayev, ruined any good will abroad for Chechnya and generated an effective media blockade as journalists ceased travelling there; rising political and even military pressure by rogue Islamist rebel groups on the freely elected nationalist president Aslan Maskhadov forced him to radicalize his position, eventually declaring a "shari'a law" no one really wanted or even understood; further decapitations of Russian captives and other atrocities, conveniently filmed by their Islamist perpetrators, continued to feed Russian anti-Chechen propaganda, with compilations of these videos being distributed to all foreign embassies at the start of the 1999 reinvasion of Chechnya to help justify the inevitable excesses of the "anti-terrorist operation."

What followed is well known: the total destruction of Groznyi, the mass killings and disappearances, the waves of refugees. What is less so, though it has been extensively documented by a handful of courageous Russian journalists, is the sinister *pas-de-deux* played by the special services and the Islamists throughout the years. This is no place to go into details, but a few examples might serve. Documents leaked by frustrated GRU officials to the Russian media revealed that the FSB paid Barayev 12 million dollars, outbidding the four telecom engineers' employers, to have them gruesomely killed in a manner maximizing the propaganda impact; in the spring of 2000, after the Federal Forces had occupied Chechnya, Chechen colleagues of mine saw Barayev – officially one of the most wanted men of Russia – freely driving through Russian checkpoints using an FSB accreditation; and it was only when his chief FSB protector, Rear-Admiral German Ugryumov, mysteriously died in May 2001 that the GRU was finally able to corner him, in an FSB base, and kill him. On a military level, when Groznyi finally fell in late January 2000, the Russian services manipulated or paid the Islamist rebel groups, which had been sent ahead to the mountains to prepare the withdrawal of the remaining forces from the city, to betray their comrades, leading to the nationalist forces being decimated during the retreat. The evidence is also strong for a form of direct complicity, or at least mutual manipulation, between the services and the Chechen Islamist commando that occupied a Moscow theater in October 2002, resulting in the death of over a hundred hostages and further discrediting president Maskhadov and his remaining guerilla forces. In spite of a succession of disastrous incidents, the most notorious being the hideous school massacre in Beslan in September 2003, this insidious strategy would bear fruit: after Maskhadov was finally killed, during a Russian operation in 2005, his successor Doku Umarov renounced the drive for national independence in favor of the creation of a pan-Caucasian Islamic Caliphate – a move that drove virtually all the remaining nationalist commanders into the arms of Ramzan Kadyrov, Putin's puppet in Chechnya, thus bringing to an effective and squalid end the long-held Chechen dream of independence. Chechen rebel activity has now been reduced to almost nothing, and Doku Umarov was killed in turn toward the end of 2013; the fact that the Islamist uprising continues unabated in neighboring regions, especially Daghestan, seems to be considered by Russia as a "manageable" problem, for now.

It would be tempting, given this history, to see the hand of Bashar al-Assad's Russian advisors in the shop-worn idea of allowing radicalized Islamist factions totally to discredit the popular revolt, all the more so as the wave of kidnappings and murders of foreign observers that accompanied the rise of the Islamists closely resembles the Chechnya model. There are also some potentially direct links. The appearance in the Syrian theater of several Chechen brigades, aligned either with Jabhat al-Nusra or Da'esh, has gained quite a bit of media attention, as has the main "Chechen" commander 'Umar al-Shishani, now a military emir of Da'esh, who is in fact a former Georgian special forces officer of mixed Christian-Muslim descent whose real name is Tarkhan Batirashvili. Less well known, however, is the fact that behind Omar al-Shishani stands a certain Isa Umarov, who left Chechnya to join him in Da'esh territory and has given him his daughter in marriage. Umarov, one of the oldest and most influential (albeit highly discrete) Chechen Islamist leaders, whose links to the KGB go all the way back to the 1980s when he was one of the founders of the Islamic Rebirth Party, the first anti-Soviet Islamist organization, is a man who played a key role in the interaction between the Russian services and the Islamists he godfathered all through the two Chechen wars; and his role within Da'esh certainly raises interesting questions. But as a Syrian friend pointed out to me, the *mukhabarat* too are old hands at these games, and have no need of lessons from their Russian patrons. Their strategic philosophy is explicitly stated in graffiti now very common around Damascus: "Assad or we burn the country."

Yet ever since the beheading of the journalist James Foley, Da'esh has become the overwhelming obsession of Western governments, clouding all other issues. The regime and its Russian friends can be proud: their goal of, if not quite rehabilitating, at least bringing al-Assad back into the game as a key player, is now within reach. It is no accident that the Syrian air force's very first bombardments of Da'esh coincided with the beginning of Coalition airstrikes (although they have now gone back to bombing moderate rebel positions, especially in Aleppo, leaving Da'esh to the Americans); nor that the French intelligence services, as *Le Monde* recently revealed, have been making overtures to Damascus and the *mukhabarat*, requesting assistance in tracking Da'esh and al-Nusra jihadists that might pose a direct threat to Europe – overtures that fortunately were disavowed by President François Hollande and his Foreign Ministry, but for how long? Even more than the fate of the broader Middle East, including Lebanon and Jordan, or the sickening executions of a few brave Western journalists and aid workers, and especially since the killing of four people at the Brussels Jewish Museum by Mehdi Nemmouche (a lost French *banlieue* delinquent who somehow ended up torturing Da'esh's Western hostages in their Aleppo dungeon before returning to Europe to become the new terrorist hero and martyr), it is the fear, even the psychosis, of another jihadi backlash against Western interests – of another September 11 or July 7 – that is driving European and US decision making. From there to working with al-Assad is only a step, no matter how much our leaders deny it. Sadly, this won't benefit the Syrian people much. A recent set of statistics published by the Syrian Network for Human Rights, usually considered one of the most reliable independent observer of the conflict, might serve as a useful reminder even if the figures are probably underestimated: as of September 2014, the regime had killed 124,752 Syrian civilians, including 17,139 children, as opposed to 831 civilians (of which 137 were children) killed by Da'esh. Our new enemy should not make us forget who is at the root of the disaster; the Syrians certainly haven't. The French journalist Sofia Amara cites, in her recent book, the new slogan chanted, with their eternal dark humor, by Syrian activists seen in a video marching through devastated streets: "What is left of the Syrian people wants the fall of the regime."

All this has taken us rather far from this small book, which does little more than open a retroactive window on a long-vanished time: a time when idealistic young citizen-activists packed themselves, in cars, around foreign journalists to protect them from snipers with their bodies; a time when the Free Syrian Army struggled to restrain Bedouin revenge killings of Alawites, on the grounds that they were playing into the regime's hands; a time when FSA soldiers could still joke about bin Laden and Zarqawi without anyone taking it too seriously; a time when, in spite of the daily death toll and the rising levels of violence, a positive outcome – one in which a state with something approaching rule of law and popular participation might be established within the Syrian borders – was still possible. When I returned from Homs, in early February 2012, I was invited to brief the then French Foreign Minister, Alain Juppé, together with his senior advisors. During the meeting, I outlined my most important observations: the main revolutionary forces still believed in a non-sectarian democratic Syria with equal rights for every community, including the Alawites; the regime was doing its utmost to provoke cycles of sectarian violence while the FSA was frantically trying to contain them; born out of despair, the Islamist temptation was growing, but had yet to gain any serious ground (Jabhat al-Nusra had in fact been founded just a few weeks earlier, but few people knew that yet). I also issued a warning:

while the revolution was struggling to contain its nega-
tives forces, this was a losing battle; if al-Assad was not
overthrown soon – something that would only be possible
with strong Western support, including the provision of
sophisticated weaponry and possibly the enforcement of a
partial or even total no-fly zone over Syria – the center
would not hold, and worse forces would emerge, driving
the revolution into the arms of criminals and Islamist rad-
icals. To my surprise, Juppé completely shared this
analysis; but alone, he added, without the participation of
its American and British allies, France could do nothing.
Inaction is always easy, but is rarely a wise course of
action. We have seen the results.

Nothing could be more emblematic of the descent into
hell of the Syrian revolution than the fates of our Homsi
activist friends. The dream had been dreamed by many;
but what happened to them when it turned into a nightmare? I only received news of them quite recently, from
'Orwa Nyrabia, a Syrian filmmaker and producer now
living in exile in Berlin, whom I first met in the al-Bayada
neighborhood of Homs at the home of the Sufi shaykh
Abu Brahim, a highly respected local activist. 'Orwa,
together with his friend Talal Derki, had dropped in from
Damascus on the afternoon of January 29, a few hours
after a ten-year-old boy named Taha had been shot and
killed nearby by a sniper. They had already begun making
what would one day become *Return to Homs*, which Talal
directed and 'Orwa partly filmed, and images of Taha's
body, lying on the cold floor of Abu Brahim's clandestine
clinic, feature toward the beginning of the film; the brief

conversation I had that day with 'Orwa is recorded in this book.[2] Months later, on August 23, 'Orwa was arrested by the *mukhabarat* as he tried to fly out of Damascus airport to Egypt; most unusually, but fortunately for him, an international pressure campaign supported by the likes of Robert de Niro and Robert Redford succeeded in securing his release after a few months. 'Orwa went on to produce *Return to Homs*, followed by another masterpiece of the Syrian revolution, Usama Muhammad and Wiam Simav Bedirxan's *Silvered Water, Syria Self-Portrait*, which was first shown to great acclaim at the 2014 Cannes Film Festival. 'Orwa, unlike me, had never lost touch with the Homsi activists, many of whom were his dear friends, and was thus able to fill in, for me, the blanks left in my original April 2012 epilogue.

Many, of course, are dead. Abu Hanin, the Media Center activist from Baba 'Amr with whom Mani and I had so many problems, was killed together with his closest friend and rival Abu Sham in one of the battles for al-Khalidiya, some time in 2013. Bilal, the medical activist who greeted us in al-Khalidiya together with his friend Zayn, was killed in June 2013 trying to smuggle medical supplies into besieged Homs. And Shaykh Abu Brahim, after having survived the terrible siege and evacuation of Homs, was killed in June 2014, in an ordinary car crash somewhere north of the city: *maktub*, as he might have said himself. The others have fared little better. 'Ali 'Uthman, aka Jeddi, is still under detention by the *mukhabarat*, along with

---

2   See the corresponding chapter.

Usama al-Habaly (aka Usama al-Homsi), who filmed parts of *Return to Homs* together with 'Orwa and whom I certainly met, even though he is not mentioned in this book. Neither one of them, though they never wielded a weapon more dangerous than a camera, seem to have benefited from the amnesty declared by Bashar al-'Assad upon his June 2014 "re-election" for all prisoners "without blood on their hands." Abu 'Adnan, the al-Khalidiya activist who drove us around the city's besieged central neighborhoods, and whose real name is Kahtan Hassoun, went on, after Osama's arrest, to film the rest of *Return to Homs*, and is currently struggling in bitter exile in Turkey. 'Umar Talawi, the Bab as-Saba'a activist made famous by his raging YouTube and Al Jazeera speeches, was wounded in October 2013 while covering shelling in Homs, but is still alive, though he has dropped out of sight for the past few months. And some, finally, have been overwhelmed by the nightmare and now feed it. Abu Bakr – the red-bearded activist who reminded me of a cheerful Chechen, and who was considered around Khalidiya as the harmless neighborhood fool – has joined Jabhat al-Nusra, where he has carved out a sinister reputation for himself through executions and beheadings. Most tragic of all, to me, is the destiny of Abu Bilal, 'Umar Talawi's enthusiastic young friend who so passionately wielded his camera for freedom and democracy in Syria. By the end of the siege of Homs, he had joined the most radical jihadist groups and was couching all his statements in Islamist terminology; after the evacuation, he officially declared his allegiance to Da'esh, and has become one of their chief spokesmen in the Idlib region. His, of course, is but one case, and there are hundreds of activists, in Aleppo and elsewhere, who still maintain their faith in the original ideals of the revolution – indeed, many of them survived the *mukhabarat*, the snipers, and the regime bombings only to be murdered by Abu Bilal's new friends. Given what he has lived through, one could perhaps understand his choice, or his despair at least, just as one can understand when someone goes insane. But that doesn't make it any less sad.

October 2014

Preliminary Note

This is a document, not a work of literature. It is the transcription — as faithful as possible — of two notebooks I kept during a clandestine trip to Syria, in January of 2012. These notebooks were originally intended to serve as a basis for the articles I wrote when I returned. But little by little, because of the endless periods of waiting or of idleness, the countless pauses generated, during conversations, by the translation, and a certain feverishness that tends to want immediately to transform life into text, they took on a new dimension. This is what makes their publication possible. What justifies it is something quite different: the fact that they give an account of a brief moment, one, furthermore, that occurred almost without any outside witnesses, the last days of the uprising of a part of the city of Homs against the regime of Bashar al-Assad, just before it was crushed in a bloodbath that, as I write these lines, is still going on.

I would have liked to present this text in its raw form, as it was in the notebooks. But certain passages, because of the conditions under which I wrote, were too confused or fragmentary and had to be rewritten. Elsewhere, memory was tempted to compensate for lack of attention. But aside from the footnotes, and the necessary explanations or commentaries, set in italics, I have tried not to add anything.

The Syrian government, as we know, has almost completely forbidden foreign journalists from working on its territory. The few professionals who obtain a press visa are carefully guided and supervised, limited in their movements and their opportunities to meet ordinary Syrians, and subjected to all kinds of manipulations or provocations – sometimes murderous, like the one that took the life of the French reporter Gilles Jacquier. Some have been able to work on their own, either by entering with a tourist visa and then "escaping" surveillance, or by crossing the border illegally, with the support of the Free Syrian Army, as I did together with the photographer Mani. Here too, as we've seen in the past few weeks, the risks are not negligible.[3]

I got the idea for this assignment in December 2011, after my friend Manon Loizeau returned from Homs, where she had just filmed a documentary. I discussed it with the editors of the newspaper Le Monde, *who accepted the project and then suggested I team up with Mani. Mani had already spent over a month in Syria, in October and November 2011, and had*

---

3 *Note to the Verso Edition*: These words, written in the spring of 2012, were a reference to the then recent deaths of Anthony Shadid, the *New York Times* Middle East correspondent who on February 16, 2012, suffered a fatal asthma attack while being smuggled out of Syria by the Free Syrian Army; and of *Sunday Times* reporter Marie Colvin and French photographer Rémy Ochlik, killed on February 22, 2012, in a Syrian Army rocket attack against the Baba 'Amr rebel press center in Homs. Two other journalists, Edith Bouvier and Paul Conroy, were severely injured in the same attack, but survived.

published a first series of photographs, groundbreaking ones at the time. That we were able to get into Syria quickly and with relative ease, and work in Homs as freely as we did, was thanks to his contacts and his previous knowledge of the field. Faced with the near impossibility of finding a translator locally, Mani, who speaks fluent Arabic, also translated most of the conversations for me. Our report, in text and photos, was published in Le Monde *in five parts, from February 14 to 18.*

Mani, of course, appears regularly in these notebooks. Because of the clandestine conditions, we had both adopted "noms de guerre" (mine was Abu Emir), and here I keep the one Mani chose, Ra'id. Similarly, most of our Syrian interlocutors appear under pseudonyms — either the ones they chose for themselves, or ones of my own invention. Those who appear under their real names expressly authorized this. I am not, furthermore, publishing the names of the people I saw wounded or killed, from fear of possible reprisals against them or their surviving families.

This reporting would not have been possible without the trust and support granted me by Le Monde. *I would like to thank all those at the paper who took part in the project, especially Serge Michel, deputy editor-in-chief, and Gilles Paris, the international news editor. Finally, I would like to express all my gratitude and admiration for the many Syrians, civilian militants, and combatants of the Free Syrian Army, who lent us their aid, spontaneously and often at the risk of their lives.*

Monday, January 16

Tripoli, Lebanon

I arrived in Beirut on Friday, January 13. Mani joined me the next day, and immediately began telephoning his Syrian contacts to arrange our passage. Abu Brahim, a respected religious authority from the neighborhood of al-Bayada with whom Mani had stayed in November, asked his contacts in the Free Syrian Army (FSA) to organize passage for us. On Monday 16, around 5:00 PM, Mani – henceforth called Ra'id – received a phone call asking us to come to Tripoli that very night.

10:30 PM. Reached Tripoli in the rain.[4] Met at the agreed-upon spot by three strapping fellows, then brought to a nearby apartment. Unlit staircase, naked electric wires bulging from the walls. Freezing apartment, but huge and beautiful, with stone floors, paintings, and Arabic calligraphy on the walls, gilt velour furniture, a big glass chandelier. D., a young activist who came out of Homs a

---

4   A map of the border region between Tripoli and Homs can be found on p. vii, along with a map of the city of Homs and its main neighborhoods on p. viii.

week ago, is chatting on Skype, his laptop resting on a low table. "It's a bachelor's apartment, sorry!" A TV, up on a dresser, is tuned to the "People of Syria" channel, an opposition network based in Great Britain.

D. immediately talks to us about Jacquier. "The regime deliberately assassinated Gilles Jacquier in order to dissuade journalists from coming. He was killed in Akrameh, a pro-regime Alawite neighborhood, in al-Jadida, in front of the Al-Butul supermarket. The false information about the place of the attack was broadcast by the regime and a traitor journalist." He means Muhammad Ballout, from the BBC's Arabic service, a Lebanese member of the Syrian Social Nationalist Party. The BBC apparently apologized.

Gilles Jacquier, a France 2 reporter, was killed in Homs on January 11 in a bombing, during a press trip that was organized and supervised by the Syrian authorities. The Syrian government and the opposition accuse each other of his death. During our stay in Syria, many of our interlocutors would talk to us about Jacquier's death, and would try to convince us, without ever presenting any concrete proof, of the regime's guilt.

Men arrive. The leader, A., our smuggler, is a bearded, stocky, smiling guy in a black tracksuit, two cellphones in hand.

D. continues to talk about Jacquier. The opposition considers him a *shahid*,[5] like all the other victims of the regime.

---

5   Martyr.

Last Thursday was celebrated as "The Day of Loyalty to
Gilles Jacquier" on the revolution's Facebook page; every
day receives a name, not just the Fridays. D. praises him:
"He came to bear witness to the martyrdom of the Syrian
people." The revolutionary coordination committees are
collecting proof that Gilles Jacquier was killed by the
regime. He quotes a few at random: the *shabbiha*[6] running
rampant in Homs come from Akrama and the neighboring
areas; it's very hard for people from the opposition to enter
those places. The university, to the west, is a military zone.
Finally, Syrian television mentioned mortar shells: D.
affirms that the FSA does not have any mortars, or heavy
weaponry of that kind. It's one of the first things he talks
about, and he insists strongly on it. The smuggler interrupts and we discuss different types of mortar; for him a 60
mm mortar, which weighs 90 kg, is too heavy to carry for a
soldier. I don't agree and we quibble over the details.

Dinner: a copious meal, from a take-out place, chicken,
hummus, falafel, salad. The smuggler's nickname is
Al-Ghadab, "Fury." "They've called me that since the
beginning of the revolution, but I laugh all the time!" His
two friends are Lebanese, smugglers who will get us past
the Lebanese security checkpoints tomorrow. Then Fury,
who is from Homs, will bring us to the city. There are four

---

6   Pro-regime henchmen, often Alawites. In the 1990s the term referred
to the Alawite mafia rampant on the Syrian coast, under the protection of the
authorities, before Bashar al-Assad had them dissolved when he came to
power in 2000. The term was taken up again to refer to civilians recruited by
the regime, from the very beginning of the events, to take part in the
repression.

stages, it will take a day, a day and a half. Car to the border, then a few kilometers on motorbike, then car again.

Manon Loizeau had explained to me that she had had to cross a minefield to get into Syria. I ask Fury about this.

In principle, we shouldn't have to go through the minefields. There are other ways to cross, which work well, except for unforeseen circumstances. Fury himself only had to pass through the mines once. But even if we have to, it's not a problem: the FSA has de-mined a three-meter wide corridor through the middle of the mined area, two weeks after the Army put them there two months ago. One guy lost his legs in the process. The men laugh: "Boom!" and make a gesture imitating the wings of an angel, hands at their shoulders. The corridor is marked with stones, and it is regularly used by smugglers. Fury: "If we have to cross it, I'll go in front of you. Your lives are more important than mine." Grandiloquent but sincere.

Tuesday, January 17

Tripoli – border – al-Qusayr

5:30 AM. Call of the muezzin. Very beautiful, massively amplified, cuts through the night.

6:50 AM. Waking up. Bleary gray morning. In the living room, the two Lebanese smugglers wait in silence.

7:30 AM. Departure. White minivan, like a little bus, with a video screen. One of the Lebanese men drives. Video and music at top volume. We weave through the Tripoli traffic in the pouring rain. Then suburbs, factories. We'll have to make a long detour, snow is blocking the passes. There are also two Lebanese Army checkpoints we have to avoid. The shortest road, normally, is the northern one.

Passage through the Mount Lebanon range: tortuous road, threadbare landscape, little clouds clinging to the peaks, a soft snow that melts on the vehicle. Checkpoint passed without stopping. At one point we pick up a hitchhiking soldier, I'm lying down, I open one eye and then go back to sleep. We leave the soldier in a Shiite hamlet swarming with soldiers. I am woken up on a long dirt road in the middle of a desert plain, with Mount Lebanon hidden in clouds on one side and a village nestled at the foot of little hills on the other. Syria is in front of us. We pass farmers, sheep. Finally, after a few bumpy kilometers, we join a road, having skirted round the Lebanese General Security border post. Money changes hands: Fury gives $700 to the Lebanese men, for us maybe, then another $1,000, for purchases it seems – to smuggle some mortars, perhaps? On the road there is a Hezbollah mosque, we're near a Shiite village; as in the Beqaa, this area is a mosaic of faiths.

Fury: "Most Sunni villagers support the uprising, with some exceptions; for the Shiites, it's the opposite." On the road, we join three young guys with two beat-up motorcycles, old Chinese bikes. They're local farmers, with calloused hands. We bid our Lebanese friends farewell, settle at three to a bike, and start weaving on dirt roads between houses and fields. Children in hand-me-down clothes with running noses, sheep, beehives, a boy galloping on horseback. A few kilometers and then we arrive at a house, already over the border. We passed right between a Lebanese Special Forces and a Syrian Army position. But the border is an in depth concept, not a line.

The "border" is not limited to the line drawn on the map, but exists for dozens of kilometers on either side, thanks to a system of both fixed and mobile checkpoints. On the other hand, for the people who live in this sort of village straddling the line it doesn't really exist, or else merely as an economic concept, allowing them to carry out business by traveling from one side to the other.

Now we're at the home of some people – farmers with their families. Coffee, the fathers stroke their sons. A radio summons, everything is ready, we leave. Crossing.[7] A few hundred meters further, another house where we're led into the reception room. Text message in English on Ra'id's cell: MINISTRY OF TOURISM WELCOMES YOU IN SYRIA. PLEASE CALL 137 FOR TOURISM INFORMATION OR COMPLAINTS. Welcome to Wonderland. It is dead noon.

A wealthy house, beautiful living room with floral-patterned rugs and divans, made of synthetic material. Big oil-burning stove, *sobia* in Syrian, and a gas lamp. Ample meal served on a tray by some boys. No women visible. Our host explains the FSA organization for the sector: the al-Qusayr units are part of the al-Faruk *katiba*[8] of Baba 'Amr, commanded by 'Abd ar-Razzaq Tlass, a *mulazim awwal,*[9] the first officer to have defected from the government Army.

We already know that to get into Homs we will probably have to pass through Baba 'Amr, a neighborhood in the southwest part of the city completely controlled by the FSA. Abu Brahim, who organized our passage, lives in al-Bayada, in the north of the city. So we ask some questions about the situation in Baba 'Amr and the border zone.

---

7 Note *to the Verso edition*: We entered Syria by driving on motorcycles through a Syrian Army checkpoint where the soldiers, silent accomplices of the FSA, simply ignored us. At the time I first published this book, this information was too sensitive to reveal.

8 Battalion.

9 Lieutenant.

Our host: Baba 'Amr is an FSA bastion because it's a large neighborhood and communicates with the orchards above the Orontes. It is surrounded, but the Army doesn't enter it. There are FSA units in other neighborhoods – al-Khalidiya, al-Bayada, etc. – but less important ones since those neighborhoods are smaller and more easily controllable by the security forces.

There are no demonstrations in the border villages. They want to preserve calm so as not to attract the *mukhabarat*[10] and risk disturbing the smuggling. Further on, near al-Qusayr, the FSA has units and is attacking the Army and the security forces.

There have already been two raids by the Army and the *mukhabarat* in the village. They searched houses to locate some wanted people. They didn't find anything, and left without causing any problems. Here, they came to the front door and asked questions, but didn't come in.

Me: "Aren't you afraid for your children?" Him: "I'm only afraid of God." He trusts his kids, who are listening to our conversation. "They know how to keep quiet."

Women take part as well, giving emergency medical care, helping to transfer the wounded, etc.

Him: "We've lived under oppression for a long time. It's a police system where no one trusts anyone." As a Sunni,

---

10   "Intelligence." This term, like "security forces," is used in a generic way, in Syria, to designate four different services: *Shu'bat al-Mukhabarat al-'Askariyya*, the Military Intelligence Department; *Idarat al-Amn al-'Amm*, the General Security Directorate, often still called by its old name, State Security; *Idarat al-Amn al-Siyasi*, the Political Security Directorate; and *Idarat al-Mukhabarat al-Jawiyya*, the Air Force Intelligence Directorate, the most powerful and feared of all.

he feels discriminated against. The good jobs are reserved for Alawites. "There's no justice, you can't demand fair treatment. Arrested people disappear, no one has access to them, there is no news of them." His son wanted to join the police, and tried for three years without success. He thinks it's because he is Sunni.

At first they just wanted reforms, more freedom. Then, confronted with the repression, things went further.

———

Departure, toward 1:00 PM. Fury arrives with a pickup and we squeeze in, all three up front. Phone call from Baba 'Amr: some agitated guys say we can't enter, they can't receive journalists, the smuggler has to take us back to Lebanon. Ra'id calls his contacts and things settle down little by little. We leave.

The reticence of certain opposition activists in Baba 'Amr to welcome more journalists was very strong during this period, even though this would completely change later on when the massive bombing of the neighborhood started. It would be a source of constant friction during our stay in Baba 'Amr.

A mixed region, with villages of different faiths. We enter an agricultural zone controlled by the FSA. We pass a commander in a pickup, then a checkpoint with a soldier, then, on a bridge, a bigger checkpoint. Endless minibuses and little pickup trucks, coming and going from Lebanon, smugglers. The checkpoint searches them, lets them pass. Another road, another phone call from Homs. Some kid hollers over the VHF,[11] a soldier's son playing. Fury, along with the radio, keeps a grenade next to the steering wheel. If we run into a flying checkpoint, he won't stop.

We leave the highway for a dirt road: we are reaching one of the checkpoints that surround al-Qusayr. We avoid it by taking dirt roads followed by derelict fields inhabited by Bedouins in military tents. On a small road, we pass 300 meters away from the checkpoint, which Fury shows me, laughing. We enter al-Qusayr, a city of 70,000 inhabitants, crumbling cement two-story houses, painted in faded pastels. Rain, passersby, motorbikes. We dodge through little streets before reaching the smuggler's house. It is 2:00 PM, it's taken six and a half hours from Tripoli.

In fact, we are not at Fury's home but the home of a friend of his, Abu Amar. Small guest room, a computer and printer, the oil stove. There are several people, we are served tea and cakes. A guy turns up with a Kalashnikov; this neighborhood is "free." A mosque loudspeaker starts up: a martyr will be buried following the afternoon prayer, the imam announces. This morning they have already buried two. All three were killed together, in Homs. Discussion to find out if we can go. They don't want us to because funerals can easily turn into a demonstration and the Army might shoot; also, they're afraid of being spotted with us.

After making inquiries, it turns out the dead man has already been buried. His name was Ahmad I., aged fifty.

---

11   A small portable radio, also known as a walkie-talkie.

Families sometimes bury their dead before the imam's announcement, to avoid trouble.

The three men were killed in the pro-regime Shammas neighborhood in Homs. A group of *shabbiha* entered the supermarket in the Sakan al-Shabbab mall where they worked, and executed them simply because they came from al-Qusayr. The two others were between twenty-five and thirty, and were named Rasul I. and Muhammad H. Rasul is related to Ahmad.

A few shots in the distance. Maybe warning shots, in anticipation of the demonstration?

––––––

The public hospital in al-Qusayr, near the cemetery, is occupied by the security forces. There are snipers on the roof.

A visit to a clandestine medical unit set up inside a house. Basic supplies – syringes, saline solution, compresses – are offered by families and pharmacies. Plastic on the floor over the rug, for the blood?

The doctor who had been in charge, 'Abd ar-Rahim Amir, was killed in Rastan two months ago. He was cornered in a health center by the military *mukhabarat* and executed. Nurses were arrested. Here, there's one doctor and one nurse left. It's the only center in town; there's another one 12 kilometers away, across the river, in a tent.

First aid only. People die here of basic wounds, of hemorrhages. They try to evacuate the more seriously injured to Lebanon, but it's difficult. They receive one or two wounded a day, injured during demonstrations or at night by gunshots. There is an unofficial curfew and snipers shoot at people at night. Wounds are mostly to the upper regions, thorax, and head. Also people released from prison: tortured, bones broken.

———

Center of the neighborhood. Young people gather for a demonstration. Flag of the revolution: black, white, and green with three red stars. One or two guys with Kalashnikovs serve as watchmen. The neighborhood is protected by the FSA. The Army doesn't enter, but fires from the hospital and the town hall.

Free Syrian Army: *al-Jaysh as-Suri al-Hurr.*
Regular Army: *al-Jaysh al-Assadi,* "the Army of the Assads."

We pass close to the town hall, a big Soviet-style building, four floors, with bluish reflecting windows all smashed up. The FSA tried to attack it but didn't succeed, it was too well fortified. The RPGs[12] served no purpose, and they didn't want to use mortars as the town hall is surrounded by civilian houses. On the roof and on every floor are sniper

———

12 *Ruchnoy protivotankovy granatomyot,* "portable antitank grenade launcher," also known in English as a "rocket-propelled grenade." A Soviet-era weapon, widespread these days, and coveted by guerillas the world over; a kind of bazooka, which shoots a rocket with an explosive shaped charge.

nests. We approach the town hall down a long street, straight toward the building. In theory the snipers only shoot at night. Here, everything is calm.

Further on, a garden that serves as a cemetery for the *shahids*. Burials in the normal cemetery had become too dangerous, the Army regularly shot at the demonstrations that formed.

––––––

4:00 PM. An old man dies of old age and will be buried quickly. Often the young (*shabbab*) use the slightest pretext for a demonstration, and even if the old man is not a *shahid* his burial could be one. But since he is not a *shahid* it will be in the normal cemetery. So there could be shooting.

We make the rounds of the city, accompanied by a guy on a motorbike. Again, we pass just by the town hall, 200 meters from a big Army post at the corner of the building. In the street of the souk, all the shops are closed; we meet an ex-doctor from the hospital who resigned three months ago when the Army occupied the structure and sent the doctors and the staff to another, inadequate building. He says that since the beginning of the troubles, in August, there have been 120 deaths in al-Qusayr. Our friend Fury shows us a video on his cellphone: the first *shahid* from al-Qusayr, in August, on the eleventh day of Ramadan, naked aside from some dirty underwear, his body riddled with bullets, his leg torn open, a butchery.

We catch up with the funeral but there won't be a demon-stration. We are introduced to some of the al-Qusayr civilian coordinators. We chat, the guys joke, laugh, a very deep laughter, fed by everything that's happening. A joyful despair, perhaps.

———

6:30 PM. Magnificent dish of rice, meat, chicken, grilled almonds, *kapsi* served with *labneh*. Political discussion. The main objective of our host, Abu Amar: "I want a civil State" – "What does that mean for you?" – "A state where the Army and the security services can't interfere in peo-ple's lives. Here, even to get married you need permission from the *mukhabarat*. A state where everyone has freedom of religion, as he likes. Look at me, I let my beard grow, I've had trouble because of that. If more than five people gather, it's forbidden, you can be arrested. It's the same for Christians, they can be arrested too if more than five of them meet." Fury: "Salafi Christians!" They dream less of democracy, a concept that no doubt is very vague to them, than of the rule of law.

———

7:00 PM. Demonstration in the street, in front of the neighborhood mosque, protected by the FSA and lit up by spotlights. 300 people? There's one every day. Opposition flags, drums, chanting and dancing, all of it very beautiful and joyful. The men dance in long lines, holding each other by the shoulder. Slogans: "Bashar, we don't know who you are, Muslim or Jew!" "Bashar, you have a giraffe's neck!"

An information guy[13] is filming from the mosque roof. Off to one side, women and children watch, and also sing. But only the men demonstrate.

I climb on the roof to join the information guy. His name is M. and he speaks a little English. He shows me a video of a corpse. One of the dead from the supermarket in Homs, perhaps? It isn't clear to me, and M.'s English isn't good enough. The dead man is about forty to fifty years old, with a moustache, a bullet in his foot, and his arm cut off with a knife. The arm, if I understand correctly, was cut off when he was still alive; he was killed afterwards. In the film, the father of the dead man is crying.

M: "The demonstration is a *dhikr*."[14] But there are Christians as well. He introduces me to one, a thirty-four-year-old man, pro-opposition. This latter proudly shows me the cross he wears around his neck. He is wanted and can no longer sleep at home. At the funeral for the three men killed in Homs there were about fifty Christians, I'm told.

M. insists on the interconfessional unity of the Syrians, as does the Christian man. "We've lived together for over a hundred years. It's Bashar, when he came into power, who stirred up problems between us. So that France and other countries would say, 'The Christians must be protected.'"

M. again: "This country is for everyone, and God is for us."

---

13   The activists in charge of information belong to the local coordination committees, the coordination bodies of the revolutionary activists. They are in charge of filming every demonstration, with a sign showing the place and date, to counter the propaganda of the regime seeking to minimize the scale of the uprising. They also film bombardments, wounded, dead, and all other forms of brutality.

14   Mystic Sufi ceremony, which often takes the form of ecstatic dances.

Slogans: "Bashar, get out, you and your dogs!" "Bashar, we're the ones from Syria, not you!" The lines of dancers do adopt the form of a *dhikr*, but without any religious content. Very joyful demonstration in any case.

It's better not take out my notebook in the street. People immediately become paranoid.

———

8:15 PM. Night expedition to a farm outside of al-Qusayr, in the countryside, to meet an officer. A smiling boy welcomes us into the reception room; he is seventeen, and is helping out the FSA, but doesn't take part in the action.

The boy counts bullets while we wait. 9 mm, and ammunition in Israeli cases, 200 7.62 mm cartridges in belts for machine guns, with a tracer every five rounds.

Shots in the night, the *dushka* of a BTR[15] next to the hospital. A few volleys.

Ra'id discusses crossing the border with Fury. Fury explains that he used the Lebanese's minivan because of us. Usually he takes the bus. It cost them several hundred dollars, but he refuses payment from us.

————

15 *Bronetransportyor*, "Armored [troop] transport," a Russian-made military vehicle with eight wheels and a turret usually armed with a 14.5 mm machine gun. In Russian military slang, the *dushka* ("little soul") designates the *Degtyaryova-Shpagina Krupnokaliberny* or DShK (hence the nickname), a 12.7 mm machine gun. But it is possible that the Syrians use the same name, pronounced their own way, for the 14.5 mm.

Discussion about the cost of weapons. Fury: an RPG costs $2,500 (including transport); a rocket, $650. A Kalashnikov, a *Rusi* as they call it here, $1,800. A 60 mm mortar, $4,500, a 60 mm mortar shell, $150. An 80 mm mortar, $7,500.

The FSA gets most of its ammunition through attacks. They don't have much money. Sometimes, sympathizers from the regular Army give them some. Sometimes the FSA buys some from them, but it's rare.

Fury thinks the regime won't fall peacefully. It will have to be overturned by force. The number of deserters is increasing. He estimates the number of deserters in the Homs area at 10,000.

Fury is wanted. The FSA bought some lists from the *mukhabarat*, his name is on one. He is twenty-eight years old. Before, he was a carpenter. In 2010, he did the little Hajj, and shows me the Jordanian and Saudi visas in his passport. He was a bachelor and was going to get married just before the start of the events. He had a choice: revolution or marriage. Now, he is on the move all the time. He doesn't do it for the money (his family is well-off), he is not a smuggler. He runs journalists, wounded, medical supplies, etc. for the FSA.

At first, he only demonstrated, but after the fourth month he got fed up with seeing demonstrators getting killed. He began to act as a runner in July, when one of the first senior officers, the *muqaddam*[16] Husayn Harmush, defected to form the first *katibas* of the FSA.

---

16   Lieutenant-Colonel.

Husayn Harmush, who had taken refuge in Turkey, was kidnapped there in August, and reappeared on Syrian television going through the confession routine: he received money from abroad, etc. According to some sources he was executed by the Air Force Intelligence Directorate at the end of January, when the FSA offered to trade him for supposed Iranian agents captured in Homs.

We drink maté, imported from Argentina. It's very common here. The officer doesn't come and finally we return to al-Qusayr, to spend the night at Abu Amar's.

Wednesday, January 18

Al-Qusayr

As we are about to go to bed, Fury or our host, I forget which, explains to us that the FSA plans to attack Army positions tonight; the counterattack will no doubt be violent, with the city being bombed and perhaps an incursion and door-to-door searches: so we should be ready to run for it, at any time.

Finally a calm night, aside from Kalashnikov volleys fired from posts around the hospital, in the air and at neighboring houses apparently, to intimidate people. The planned attack didn't take place, nor did our anticipated evacuation, we were able to sleep all through the night. Around 3:00 or 4:00 AM the electricity came back, and all the neon lights with it. The only one awakened, I was the one to turn them off.

Heavy, elaborate dreams, I shyly meet Michel Foucault, not in great shape but still alive, and try to set up a lunch with him. Streets. The cracks in the asphalt are full of coins, some as big as 2 euros. At the university I have swimming class, but don't know if I manage to make it.

[*Discussion with some visitors.*] Around al-Qusayr, four or five days ago, the BMPs[17] and BTRs were replaced by T-62s and T-72s.[18] They're not very visible, more or less hidden, because of the agreement with the Arab League, but they're there. The FSA thinks it's in anticipation of an assault. One man: "People are very afraid, they fear the Army." For him, the presence of the FSA makes not only our visit possible, but also the demonstrations, the burials. Previously, the security forces patrolled, entered houses, arrested people.

Fury says: the groups in Homs don't want any more journalists and have agreed on that. We'll be the last group, after, *khalas*, finished. He doesn't really know why: anticipation of a big attack, the death of Gilles Jacquier?

For Fury, Ra'id explains to me, we are on *amana*, a term that could be more or less translated as "deposit"; he is responsible for us up to Homs.

Our host, yesterday, sent his wife and children home to her parents. "So as not to disturb you, so we'd be at ease." In any case women are invisible. A world of men. From time to time you see a woman in the street, veiled but with her face showing. Yesterday Fury, in the car, spoke with the mother of a martyr, and with the wife of D., the boy

---

17   *Boyevaya Mashina Pekhoty*, "Infantry Combat Vehicle," a light Soviet-designed armored vehicle, amphibious and with treads, armed with a 30 mm gun.

18   Heavy Soviet-era tanks.

from Tripoli. At the demonstration a few women stood to one side, in a group, near a gate, singing too, but apart from the men.

Arrival of an FSA officer, Abu Hayder, a *mulaẓim awwal* and native of al-Qusayr. Jeans, military jacket with markings (two stars), thick beard, worker's hands. He served for six or seven years in the Army. At the beginning of the events he was based in Dara'a. He had more or less believed the party line – that of a conspiracy against Syria – but soon came around. He deserted in August, during Ramadan, but without announcing it officially on TV. A friend of his had been wounded, by some *shabbiha*, during a peaceful demonstration in which he took part. He brought the friend to the emergency ward, but he died. At that time the hospital was still functioning. At the hospital, his dead friend was filmed, then shown on Dunya TV,[19] and presented as an innocent demonstrator killed by terrorists. This lie revolted Abu Hayder and was the trigger for his desertion. At that time, there was no FSA in town.

Abu Hayder had belonged to a special unit of the Administration of Chemical Warfare; he was in charge of firing colored smoke bombs from a special vehicle on to buildings that needed to be spared during shelling, to "mark" them.

Asserts that around August, he witnessed aerial bombardments of civilian habitations and the population

---

19 The private TV network of Rami Makhlouf, a powerful cousin of Bashar al-Assad.

(demonstrators) in Dara'a. There were already units of deserters, the future FSA, and the Army was prevented from intervening, so they sent planes.

Fury is going to take us to the the *autostrad*, where Abu Brahim will send someone to pick us up to take us directly to al-Bayada. Whereas this morning it was again planned that we would enter the city through Baba 'Amr, they again categorically said no. Energetic conversations on the cellphone. Yesterday, al-Bayada and al-Khalidiya were shelled by tanks, which is rare. Very tense situation.

FSA in Baba 'Amr convinced that the *shabbiha* and the security forces are going to target foreign journalists in order to boost the official case for terrorism. That's why they don't want us there. They think it's too risky.

Furious discussions on the phone with Abu Brahim, constantly cut off, to arrange the rendezvous on the *autostrad*. Abu Hayder talks with the loudspeaker on, he yells and waves the phone in front of his mouth.

D.'s cellphone: photos of babies, of friends, of summer expeditions where people smoke *narghiles* by the river's edge, of an Uzi with silencer, of a camouflaged pickup truck with a machine gun mounted on the back, of a spanking-new Mercedes . . .

The negotiations continue. Abu Brahim's plan is impossible: too far, too dangerous. We have to enter through Baba 'Amr, there's no choice. The people there agree, but only if they can transfer us right away to Abu Brahim.

Noon. Visit to an FSA farm with Abu Hayder. A dozen men in uniform, most of them wearing balaclavas, with AKs. A white pickup, Toyota Hilux, with a 14.5 mm *dushka* mounted in back, and stickers of the al-Faruk *katiba* on the doors. The guys pose for a photo with a flag, the *dushka*, and some RPGs, in balaclavas or *keffiyehs*.

Then they pose again in the farm, all wearing balaclavas, with their weapons and the *katiba* sticker. A feeling of novice guerillas; novices in PR, above all.

Abu Ahmad, who commands the north zone of al-Qusayr. An officer who deserted, a *mulazim*.[20] Thick beard, moustache shaved, Islamist-style. He had quit the Army before the uprising, because of a personal conflict, and joined the FSA at its start. In April already, they were trying to organize themselves militarily, but there weren't yet any confrontations.

They have contacts with ex-soldiers and with active officers. Many accomplices in the Army, sympathizers, officers who help them, especially by providing them with ammunition. They obtain half their ammunition that way. Abu Hayder was able to desert thanks to such complicities.

The *naqib*[21] who founded and commanded the *katiba* was named Abu 'Abayda. He was killed on September 28. A soldier shows me a video of his corpse on his cellphone.

---

20 Second lieutenant.
21 Captain.

I am also shown a video of the entrance of T-72s into al-Qusayr, on December 16, on tank transports, many of them. Then photos of a destroyed tank. Then a video of an attack on a convoy, several vehicles are burning, an RPG destroys one of them, voices holler *Allahu Akbar!* All that took place on the 16th, they attacked as soon as the tanks arrived. They say they destroyed three tanks and nine BMPs. The armored vehicles didn't catch fire right away, and they recovered thirteen corpses of soldiers, along with seven prisoners. The next day, they forced a government driver to take the bodies back to the Army. That's when the soldiers retaliated by shelling the city, killing thirty.

On the same phone, a photo of Zarqawi with Usama bin Laden. Ra'id: "Where have we landed?" – They laugh: "It's just that we like them."

Videos also of their *shahids*, naked, with only their sex covered. Close-ups on the wounds. Exhibition of the martyred body.

The officers continue: the *katiba* rarely intervenes. They control al-Qusayr; the checkpoints stay bunkered, and don't bother them. They attack only during Army operations, when it attempts a maneuver. The Army can no longer arrest people, unless they make a big incursion.

Two months ago, the FSA managed to take the town hall, but the Army returned and dislodged them. For the past two weeks, they've had an agreement with the officer in command of the town hall. Out of fear of another attack his snipers have stopped shooting. The FSA move around freely with their pickups; the soldiers see them but don't shoot.

Here, no one has announced his defection officially. They live at home or want to be able to go home, and don't want any problems for their families. Hence the balaclavas.

Many deserters who join the FSA, individually or in groups, have themselves filmed with their faces uncovered, with their Army card held in front of them; these films are then put online on YouTube, as proof of the collapse of the Army's morale and the rise in power of the FSA.

A soldier narrates: he was a *raqib*[22] in Dara'a, in command of a small Army unit. He witnessed a massacre of eleven civilians next to Laraa, near Dara'a. The *naqib* Manhell Slimane ordered the massacre, together with *naqib* Randi. He claims that only the two officers fired, on their own, without asking the soldiers. No security forces with them. Among the victims, an eleven-year-old boy.

In Dazil, the Army had surrounded the city with 200 tanks, with orders to shoot at any vehicles that left, while the security forces and the *shabbiha* were killing. He says he fired in the air. Says there were Iranians with the *shabbiha* – they spoke a foreign language and did the same thing as the others.

His friend, a T-52[23] machine-gunner, had received the order to shoot at a roof where there were some civilians, and was liquidated because he refused. He was shot in the back. The soldier himself was with the signals unit a little

---

22   Sergeant.

23   Medium-sized Soviet tank, a completely obsolete model.

further on, he didn't see who fired. His friend was from Homs, his name was Mahmud F.

Another guy is introduced to us as a deserter from the Air Force *mukhabarat*, a simple soldier. He witnessed how they practiced torture, and deserted for that reason. But he doesn't show his card, saying it's at his house.

He says there are several ex-*mukhabarat* in ar-Rastan. Others fled to Jordan.

On the way back, in the car. Abu Hayder explains that Zarqawi is his idol, because he came to Iraq to confront Iran and the Shiites. Abu Oday, who is driving, moderates: "But here, in Syria, it's not the same at all."

————

[*At the home of Abu Amar.*] Meeting with Abu Nizur, the doctor in charge of the medical tent near the border. He speaks a little English. "It's quiet here. Nearly romantic."

The doctors who take care of the wounded are followed by the secret police. It's very dangerous. There hasn't been a hospital in al-Qusayr for two months, ever since the national hospital was occupied by the Army. That's when he set up the tent. They receive people with heavy injuries from Baba 'Amr, and try to transfer them to Lebanon. They also have a big problem with pregnant women, Homs is the only place now where you can do caesarian sections. And the city isn't always accessible.

The medical unit in al-Qusayr – the one we saw – has been open for two or three weeks. They also plan on opening another one between the town and the tent.

Abu Nizur is a general practitioner, but he has learned a little surgery on the job. "See one, do one." He can do operations of the abdomen, basic things. The *mukhabarat* are looking for him, but haven't bothered his family. He is not paid, but the people and his family help him. He is often so overworked that he doesn't even ask the names of his patients, and keeps no records. Some days he treats up to twenty patients, and he is alone.

The Army often aims at the head or chest, and some wounded die from lack of care: "Sometimes we see the patient die in front of us, and we can't do anything." He can't do the necessary surgery, or evacuate them to Lebanon. The border is very hard to cross. Sometimes you have to wait an hour or two, sometimes it's closed. Some patients die on the border itself, others are brought back to the tent and die there. What's more it takes four hours from the tent to Tripoli, which is often too long.

———

3:00 PM. Demonstration. Same place as last night, twice as many people. A hundred or so women as well, together on the side. The same chanted slogans, the same dances in a line, arms on shoulders, to the music of drums. Little babies or children on the shoulders of their fathers, sometimes with a flag. The women sway to the rhythm and clap their hands. All veiled, some with the lower part of the face also masked, a few women wearing *niqab* off in a corner. Children, including little girls, also chant slogans into the microphone, leading the crowd. Sometimes they're religious slogans.

Afterwards, a tour of the town on motorbike. The FSA checkpoints for the demonstration, the place where one of the tanks was destroyed, a nail-bomb impact.[24] Sunny but cold afternoon, pink tints in the sky, migrating birds wheel in a flock above the houses.

At the crossroads leading off to Lake Qattinah, we are again told about the fighting on December 16. The armored vehicles tried to enter al-Qusayr through this crossroads. The first night, there were six T-62s in a column, without infantry, and the FSA destroyed one of the tanks. Two days later, the Army attempted a second incursion, with two tanks accompanying a pickup truck. The tanks were destroyed and the pickup captured; the six prisoners all joined the FSA.

———

[*At the home of Abu Amar.*] 5:30 PM. Fury arrives with a guy from Baba 'Amr, Ibn Pedro. He was sent by the neighborhood's FSA to guide us there. An hour ago, at nightfall, a friend of Fury's was killed at a flying checkpoint. He was a soldier who had deserted from State Security two months ago. He was in a vehicle with a friend, they managed to turn around and flee through the trees, then on foot, but he

---

24 Usually, the term "nail bomb" refers to improvised bombs, filled with nails or other pieces of metal, typically used by Afghan or Iraqi insurgents. But the Syrians use the term to designate a type of shell that instead of bursting into fragments, like an ordinary mortar shell, disperses a volley of small pellets, as from a shotgun. I was unable to identify this ammunition, often used in Homs. The wounds it leaves in the body, little round holes, are easily recognizable.

was hit in the back by a bullet. It happened in the zone we passed through yesterday, not far from the FSA checkpoint on the bridge, where the smugglers were crossing. The checkpoint guys managed to recover the bodies.

News: there was an observation plane over the zone, with night vision equipment from Iran.

Abu Amar: "The Army is corrupt, it's an army of thieves, anyone who can pay doesn't go, only the poor get drafted. It's an incompetent army, which doesn't work. All it does is make the Alawite community grow fatter."

He himself was a non-commissioned officer for three years. Before the events, the Army wasn't ready, had no sophisticated communications or observation equipment, etc. They've had Iranian equipment only since the start of the revolution.

The Army is in a state of complete decay.

6:30 PM. The nurse we met yesterday at the health unit was taken at a checkpoint. By chance, he wasn't wanted. The center we saw yesterday has already been evacuated, all the equipment taken away.

Ra'id explains the rituals to me: the *shahid* is not washed, he is buried in his own blood. He is stripped, and at that point often filmed or photographed, to document the wounds, and for memory as well no doubt. Then he is rolled up in a shroud. If possible he is buried after the noon prayers, sometimes they wait till the night after his death. The body is exhibited in front of the wall of the *qibla* and people pray over it, always standing, without genuflecting, repeating *Allahu Akbar* ten times with the imam.

9:00 PM. Fury and Ibn Pedro. Jokes about the whiskey we're drinking, they say they'll slit our throats. Ra'id: "So it's true what Bashar says about Salafi terrorists!" Big guffaws. They confirm to us that we'll be able to enter Baba 'Amr, but we'll be the last. The FSA thinks that certain correspondents – two Englishmen? – were regime spies.

During my stay in Homs, I heard this story about journalist-spies in numerous variations. Each time, the nationality varied – Moroccans, Germans, Italians – but there were always two of them. It seems to refer to a specific incident, but I could never get any more details.

Fifteen days ago the Army came here, to Abu Amar's house, and stole all the mattresses, the blankets, the fuel oil, all the food, and broke the air conditioner. Abu Amar had to buy everything again. Curiously, the soldiers left the television.

Around 11:00 PM, people climb up to their roofs and start the *takbir*:[25] everyone begins chanting *Allahu Akbar!* You can hear it far away. Inevitably, the Army checkpoints begin firing. It's like that every night.

---

25   The word designates the phrase *Allahu Akbar*, "God is the greatest."

Thursday, January 19

Al-Qusayr – Baba 'Amr

A copious breakfast, hummus with meat, *musahabat* with hummus and *ful*, cheese, *labneh*, olives . . . Abu Amar: "Eat a lot, you're leaving for Tora Bora!" They laughingly suggest we be made to carry shells. Fury is all business: "I have to go see the Free Army, they have to give me some Benjamin Franklins!"

A soldier enters, wearing a balaclava, with a scarf knitted with the colors of free Syria. He deserted three hours ago, he explains. He's a *mulaẓim*, based in Damascus, who came here on leave. He is still in uniform, a camouflage jacket. His brother, a *mulaẓim* as well, is in prison for refusing to shoot at demonstrators. He's afraid for his brother, and that's why he's wearing a balaclava. He wants to join the FSA. Quickly, he shows us his face, so we can see it corresponds to his card.

Beneath his balaclava he looks tense, nervous. Shifty eyes. Our host upbraids him: "You're an officer, you should be brave. Why hide your face? An officer leads, he must show by example."

Two friends told this officer what happens in the military prisons in the suburbs of Damascus, al-Qabun, and Azzara. Officers are imprisoned there, for speaking out against the regime or for refusing to shoot. They are separated by faith, and there is no intermingling; all faiths are represented, Druze, Alawite, Christian, etc.

He comes from the Air Force, he was based at the military airport in Dumayr, a Damascus suburb. Co-pilot of an MI-8 helicopter. He confirms that helicopters were used against demonstrations, in az-Zabadani, with a 7.62 mm machine gun mounted in the door. At first it was just to frighten people, but later they fired for real.

———

11:00 AM. Departure in the rain with Fury and Ibn Pedro. No room inside the cab, so I crouch in the bed of a pickup loaded with crates of ammunition. After we leave al-Qusayr, we shift the ammunition, along with two rocket-launchers, into a slightly larger truck with a new driver. We all pile into the front, me on Ra'id's lap, next to Ibn Pedro. Fury heads off on his own. Road, then a long muddy path, jolting through fields, where we cross many trucks trying to avoid the checkpoint. Rain and hail alternate with bursts of sunlight. After a few kilometers, another village, we meet another truck, which is transporting medicine stashed in a metal false bottom, and another van. Quicker trip to a third village. On the way, discussion between the driver, Abu 'Abdallah, and Ra'id on Salafism. Abu 'Abdallah: "So, have you seen any Salafis here as Bashar says?" – Ra'id: "That depends. What do you mean by Salafis?" – "Exactly. The word means two things. The Muslims of the land of Sham[26] follow the path of moderation. To live well, they follow the example of pious ancestors, of a pious man from long ago who lived justly in Islam. That is the original meaning of Salafist. The other meaning, the Takfirist, jihadist, terrorist version, is a creation of the Americans and Israelis. It has nothing to do with us."

We arrive at a village and park next to a house, where we are welcomed by a woman and a smiling boy with a firm, confident handshake, a real little man. Wait in the reception room. The FSA has spotted Army movements and the way isn't clear. This could last a while.

Dialogue between Ra'id and Ibn Pedro. Ibn Pedro asks what we'd like to eat when we arrive in Baba 'Amr, to let them know so things will be ready. Ra'id: "Pork!" – Ibn Pedro: "We'll slaughter you a Shiite, then." – Ra'id: "See, you do have a sectarian attitude." – Ibn Pedro: "It's true, but they're the ones who started it. It's their fault."

Ibn Pedro says the FSA has prisons in Baba 'Amr, where they hold some *shabbiha*. They put them on trial in "good, due form. Those who have killed children are condemned to death." They have also done prisoner exchanges, especially when the Arab observers arrived.

He personally has seen a case of a *shabbiha* condemned and executed by firing squad. "He had killed children." Vague. "He's also the one who shot at me." Shows his wound, a bullet in the abdomen. Bullshit, in fact he was

---

26 Syria.

shot by a sniper in Insha'at a month and a half ago, and was treated in a secret clinic.

Lively discussion between Ra'id and Ibn Pedro. Ra'id reproaches Ibn Pedro for his exaggerations and distortions. He explains that as journalists, we have to report precise facts, that exaggerations don't help them, and don't help their cause.

Ra'id explains what Abu 'Abdallah said about the Salafis. There are in fact three currents: the *Made-in-USA* Takfiri-Jihadist current; the *Tablighi Jama'at* current [*founded in India in 1926*], a transnational, non-political current, whose purpose is the spread Islam through Muslim communities, closer to the Muslim Brotherhood; and the movement *Tahrir al Uqul*, "the freeing of minds," a non-political, religious, pious, and also elitist current.

Ra'id explains his plans to Ibn Pedro, who offers [*in order to let him move more freely around Homs*] to have a fake ID card made for him, with the mention *Christian*. It will take ten days, and is done in Lebanon.

The wait stretches on. Ra'id chatters, shows his photos on his computer. We drink tea. The men pray. Ra'id also shows some PDFs of his publications, quite useful for our credibility. [*I am reading Plutarch, the only book I brought with me.*] "These things and others like them will, I venture, please readers more for their novelty and curiosity, than they will offend them for their falsity" (*Life of Romulus*, XVIII). That fits well with Ibn Pedro's attitude.

The boy is a real big shot. When I ask him the way to the bathroom, he runs in front of me, shoves his mother into a room, and closes the door behind her.

Dialogue between Ra'id and Abu 'Abdallah, our driver. Abu 'Abdallah was an electrical engineer, he studied for six years at the engineering university in Damascus. In the 1990s, he was fired from his job at the Homs refinery, because he refused to collude in corrupt practices. Then he left for two years to practice his profession in the Emirates. After that, he returned to Syria and started a company. Now, he helps the FSA with logistics: transporting the wounded, weapons, and journalists.

Abu 'Abdallah questions us about the position of the French people and government, and Ra'id explains that overall they support the uprising, are aware of and condemn the regime's atrocities. Abu 'Abdallah agrees, but says that it doesn't help much; they don't see any concrete results. Ra'id explains that diplomatic pressure limits the regime's repression. "Look at what they did in Hama!" Abu Abdallah: Hama is different, that was an uprising provoked by a political movement, the Brotherhood, supported by Saddam Hussein.[27] Today it's an uprising of the people.

---

27   The destruction in February 1982 of the city of Hama by the forces of Hafez al-Assad, Bashar's father – destruction that caused between 10,000 and 35,000 deaths according to the available estimates – represented the peak of the repression of an armed uprising launched, after a long campaign of assassinations of Alawite officials, by the Syrian Muslim Brotherhood. After Hama, the Brotherhood party was banned, its members executed, and the survivors sought refuge abroad. Today they form the largest faction of the Syrian National Council (SNC), the main representative organ of the opposition.

The political movements are running to catch up and climb on to the people's shoulders. Especially the Brotherhood, the Communists, and the Salafis (the *Tahrir* kind, Ra'id points out – the other two don't exist in Syria). He feels that the political parties, for the past two months, have been trying to jump on board the moving train. The Brotherhood is a party, it wants results, political gain. This influences their actions. The Communists too, especially in Jabal az-Zawiya (in Idlib Governorate) and Salamiya (between Homs and Hama, where there are a lot of Ismaelites). The two parties are trying to build up their popular support. But the Syrian people refuse to let the movement be politicized. They accept help wherever it may come from, but it cannot be conditional.

One of the conditions of the Brotherhood, to support the movement, was that coordination be done in their name, and that the slogans come from them – that people demonstrate in their name. The movement refused. Afterwards, if there are elections, the Brotherhood will be free to run. The Syrian people did not rise up in order to demand a particular political option, but as a reaction to oppression and humiliation.

"I belong to the people who had no political consciousness. When I took to the streets, I didn't want to get rid of Bashar al-Assad. We just wanted a dignified life, to eat and be respected. But even practicing my religion is a problem. If you meet people at the mosque, to educate yourself, you will immediately have problems, you'll be seen as an Islamist opponent. All the institutions are politicized by the Ba'athists: schools, universities. The Syrian people is raised like chickens in a hen house: you have the right to eat, to sleep, to lay eggs, that's it. There's no room for thought. You live under the regime of the Ba'ath and Bashar al-Assad is our president for eternity. You can't imagine any alternative.

"The Syrian regime has no equivalent aside from North Korea. They put it into our heads that we are a great people, that we are fighting for the Arabs, against Israel, against imperialism. But they sold us, they sold the Arabs, the Palestinians, the Golan. The entire elite is abroad, why? They understood. And in Syria it's forbidden to understand."

At first, for lack of information, Abu 'Abdallah was ready to accept anything to get rid of this regime. In the first months, seeing the massacres, he would have accepted a foreign intervention. He had no political consciousness. Today, he views things more objectively. He doesn't want to replace one evil with another.

He also thinks that France, the United States, the West let the repression continue without intervening in order to keep Syria weak and protect Israeli interests. They don't want a strong, democratic Syria, with a powerful Army.

A thought earlier, in the truck: the twofold social grid. Faced with the police and security grid of the regime, people put together a counter-grid, made of civilian activists, local worthies, religious figures, and, more and more, militarized forces, the deserters who form the FSA. This counter-grid resists the other one, circumvents it, and, more and more, absorbs it (deserters, informants in the Army or the *mukhabarat*). When you travel, this grid becomes immediately visible, with changes of vehicles, relays, safe houses, constant telephone interchanges to warn about the evolution of the situation in the field.

You could say that Syrian society has split in two, that two parallel societies in deadly conflict with each other now coexist in the country. Before the revolution, there was of course passive resistance to the regime, but the people remained linked to the overall grid by numerous ties. Now, the second grid has completely broken off from the first, cutting off all ties one by one. Yet the two cannot continue to coexist and the struggle is deadly. One of the two must be defeated, and its components destroyed or reabsorbed by the other.

———

2:30 PM. The way is clear. Abu 'Abdallah and Ibn Pedro leave to check the route, and make sure there aren't any checkpoints.

3:00 PM. They return: *Yallah*. We leave the bags, they'll be brought tonight. Ibn Pedro goes in front in a first pickup with a driver; we follow five minutes behind, with Abu 'Abdallah. They have a system in case of a flying checkpoint that's a little hard to understand, since the telephone is down, no network. The first vehicle will go through, then will turn on its warning lights and a motorbike will come back to warn us. But nothing happens. We arrive in a Christian village, dominated by an immense chemical factory. When Abu 'Abdallah opens the window, a putrid smell invades the compartment: "Look, we're near a magnificent lake where tourists come, and they put a chemical factory here. Between this factory and the refinery, this region has the highest cancer rate in Syria." The lake shines in the distance, a thin blue tongue behind the town. Gray clouds cover the horizon, a fine rain begins to fall, the sun shines from below, illuminating the muddy, chaotic landscape dominated by this industrial dinosaur with its immense heaps of yellow powder. We have in fact skirted round the lake by the south, and we're driving alongside it toward Baba 'Amr and Homs.

In front of us appears the Damascus–Homs *autostrad*, elevated here, with a regular stream of traffic in both directions. I took this same highway in 2009, with my family, to go to the Crusaders' Fortress, a little farther on, along the Tartus road. Just before reaching it we turn left, after greeting a man. Ibn Pedro is waiting for us a little further on in front of a house. We get out, we'll continue on foot.

The man we greeted joins us. We say farewell to Abu 'Abdallah, who is leaving us here, and we start off just as the rain stops. The sun shines on the puddles. Ra'id walks in front with the man, toward an underpass below the highway, I follow a little farther back with Ibn Pedro. The passage shouldn't pose any problems, but it's better not to be in too large a group. The mud sticks to our boots. Ibn Pedro has me roll up my pants, a solicitous gesture since we really are ankle-deep and he doesn't want me to get dirty. We enter the underpass; just after it is an Army checkpoint. A soldier sticks his nose out, our friends exchange a few words, the soldier waves us through and we continue. Further on, there are vague industrial installations, crumbling walls made of prefabricated concrete, mud through which we keep wading. The man leaves us and veers left, we continue straight ahead with Ibn Pedro, moving away from the railroad. In front of us, beyond the tracks, there is another checkpoint: it is not "friendly" at all, but in principle, if we have passed the first checkpoint, this one has no reason to shoot at us. I can see the bunker of sandbags, beyond a plowed field through which we make a detour to avoid the sticky mud of the path. The post is 50 meters away, no more. We pass without a problem. Then we walk alongside some houses. A car is waiting for us 300 meters further on, with two fighters inside, an AK up front. We start off quickly. Little by little the urban fabric grows denser, we're on a road between two-story houses still under construction, there are people, it's Jobar, a suburb of Homs.

A little further on in the middle of a wide avenue, at an intersection, an FSA checkpoint, smiling young men, armed with Kalashnikovs. Ra'id wants to photograph them but Ibn Pedro refuses. Lively discussion, we stop, Ibn Pedro and Ra'id yelling at each other. The problem is that it's another *katiba*, and Ibn Pedro doesn't want any problems. He promises to take us back, with someone in charge probably. We go on. Narrow roads, a mixture of countryside, houses, little hamlets, we pass cars with soldiers, armed men on foot, another FSA checkpoint. They control the whole zone, here it's the orchards of Jobar and Baba 'Amr, then the first small buildings of Baba 'Amr.

The buildings are dotted with impacts, of mortar shells, RPGs, and tank shells. We pass some FSA posts, one next to a fruit and vegetable seller, with his crates lined up behind the soldiers, then in a deserted neighborhood we arrive at an FSA command post, a ground-floor apartment with a wall of sandbags on one side. A dozen soldiers, well armed, are eating a shared meal in mess tins. We leave again, the neighborhood seems empty, the evening light makes the yellow impact-riddled concrete almost beautiful. Finally we park in front of a building and are led into another ground-floor apartment where Hassan and his men are waiting for us.

4:20 PM. Explanations. This part of Baba 'Amr is called Haqura, it's the northern side of the neighborhood. All the inhabitants of Haqura have left for surrounding villages, out of 10,000 people only two families are left. Baba 'Amr might have between 120,000 and 130,000 inhabitants.

The al-Faruk *katiba*, which defends Baba 'Amr, numbers 1,500 men in all. The commander of Haqura is *muqaddam* Hassan. He says he deserted at the very start of the revolt: his house was destroyed during the beginning of the repression in Baba 'Amr. Earlier, he was posted in Damascus, in the infantry. He didn't announce his desertion: on the contrary, in order to protect his family the FSA called the Army with his phone and said they had killed him. For the Army he is dead.

His deputy Imad explains he has a relative in the Army, who instead of deserting gives them information. It's quite common, apparently.

Good mood, we eat *sfihas* with yogurt in the reception room. Ibn Pedro continues with his teasing about Salafis and whiskey. There are weapons pretty much everywhere: an M16 with a telescopic sight, a 7.62 mm machine gun with a round cartridge clip, an RPG with an Islamic flag knitted around the rocket.

Men come in and out, we drink tea. A boy brings in a 50 kg polyester bag with several Kalashnikovs inside. The officers test the mechanisms and dismantle them.

Bassel, a young man with a dark complexion, in a suit and a good shirt, speaks a little English. Fadi, a boy with a well-groomed beard and an anxious look, shows us the bullet he took in the back when he fled a checkpoint. It came out through his stomach.

Arrival of Muhammad, a young *mulazim*, with a Belgian sniper rifle, a 7.62 mm Herstal. Range of 800 meters, according to him. He's the unit specialist.

Arrival of Jeddi ("Grandfather"), one of the guys in charge of information, a friend of Ra'id since November. Laughter, slaps on the back: "No kidding, you're really here?" Jeddi also knows Manon Loizeau and Sofia Amara. He has several translators who work with him, they could help me. When Ra'id mentions whiskey, he laughingly takes out his pistol and chambers a round: "Whiskey? I'll kill you!" Everyone laughs. "It's the new dictatorship."

Jeddi suggests we leave with him and we get ready. But a dispute breaks out between Jeddi and Ra'id. Jeddi wants to supervise us twenty-four hours a day, while Ra'id wants us to stay and sleep here, with Hassan and his boys. The tone rises. "If you're not happy, go back to Beirut!" Finally Jeddi gets fed up and leaves. "If that's how it is, to hell with you." Ra'id tries to follow him to calm him down, then returns. So we're staying. Ra'id explains our position to

Hassan and Imad. In short, we get acquainted, and since the head of the Baba 'Amr translation bureau has just left slamming the door, I keep quiet as usual.

Other non-commissioned officers show up, including a redhead in a beige camouflage uniform who shouts in a voice that's too loud, as if he's drunk. He leaves, and half a dozen men head to the back of the room to pray. Brief argument about who will lead the prayer. The redhead returns, so he isn't drunk, and joins the prayer.

———

6:00 PM. We go out with Imad. Dark streets, very few cars or lights. We pass an intersection where there had been an Army checkpoint. The FSA surrounded it and cut off its supplies, then negotiated its pullout. We drive up a long avenue. There is another checkpoint at the end, but it's been vulnerable ever since the other one was evacuated, and they don't shoot out of fear of FSA reprisals.

Visit to the underground clinic in Baba 'Amr. At the entrance, stretchers, several people, women too. A long hallway divided by a curtain, with rooms along it. One serves as a pharmacy, the cupboards are full of medicines, there are some supplies on a table, with a heater balanced on top of it, blankets, on the floor lies a female anatomy mannequin, with all its organs and half the skull exposed, in one corner there are also two Kalashnikovs and a bullet-proof vest. We are served tea and I talk with a doctor, Dr. Abu 'Abdu, who speaks a little English. He was a general practitioner at the national hospital, but resigned at the beginning of the events. "Our work has improved since March. We have a pool of doctors. Our work is better now." He refuses to be photographed: if he is identified by Security his family would be threatened.

He explains: in the beginning, doctors worked house to house. Then they found this place, but there was neither equipment nor pharmacy. Little by little people brought contributions. They received medicine from Lebanon, and also from pharmacies in town.

They can do surgery here. Difficult to know at what level. They have surgeons, ketamine too. But they lack drains, surgical kits. Also, some doctors live in other parts of town, and can't come when the Army cuts off Baba 'Amr. Sometimes they have cases that require major surgery, but the specialist can't come.

They also sometimes send doctors and supplies further away, to Rastan and Telbisi.

The number of wounded varies. Some days it's three or five, wounded by snipers. If the Army shells, it can be a hundred or 150 cases. They don't keep any statistics. Three months ago the Army made an incursion, and they found an X-ray of a patient's chest with his name on it. The name was transmitted to the *mukhabarat*.

The people of Baba 'Amr can't go to the hospital because of the *mukhabarat*, and they can't go to private clinics, they're too poor. At the hospital, the *mukhabarat* arrest people, or at the very least prevent them from being treated if they learn they're from Baba 'Amr.

The discussion turns political. Abu 'Abdu: "Homs is a big city in the middle of Syria, surrounded by Shiite and

Alawite villages. And the government distributed weapons to these villages to fight the revolution. That's when the problems began, because then the demonstrators were no longer just against the government, they were against the Shiites and Alawites. That caused huge conflicts. Now, if they catch you and you're from Baba 'Amr, they kill you."

He shows me a video, set to music, found on YouTube apparently, in which we see two young men – one from al-Khalidiya, the other from Baba 'Amr – caught in Al-Zahra by some *shabbiha* and decapitated alive, with a knife. Ultra-graphic film, a huge gush of blood when the knife slices. The killers put both heads on the ground and plant the knife next to them. The second head, on the ground, is still quivering, from the blood probably. "You see this? How can we stop when they do this?" Abu 'Abdu says he knows the two boys, but he can't give me their names because their families don't know how they died.

"In the beginning, the *shabbiha* came with clubs, shouting 'Bashar, Bashar!' Then they came with weapons. The government says there is a problem between faiths, but it's the government that created this problem. The government is ready to kill people on both sides to intensify the conflict. Then Alawites come to the center of town, they kidnap women, they fuck our daughters and they film it. They put the videos on the web to say: 'See, we fuck Sunni girls.' For us this is very heavy, as Arab and Muslim people."

The doctor's face, as he speaks, is constantly agitated by tics.

He offers to introduce me to a woman prisoner who helped the *shabbiha* capture girls and rape them. She was an Alawite prostitute. They captured her in a taxi, an officer and three of his aides fled (the story is a little confused), and the girl told them everything.

A virulent argument breaks out between Ra'id and a bearded soldier, obtuse and aggressive, with a large band around his thick hair. The bearded man, Abu Bari, doesn't want to show us the girl. Says it doesn't serve any purpose. They already showed her to other media and it never got out. Ra'id, again, shouts. It's tiring to shout all day long.

In fact, Abu Bari is not a soldier but, as I would learn later, a civilian, the one in charge of this clinic. Later, we would have problems with him, and despite all the interventions of FSA officers he would categorically forbid us from setting foot in the structure again.

In the next room, well heated by radiators, two wounded are recuperating, in the care of two nurses, veiled but in green hospital uniforms. They let me photograph them after covering their faces with pieces of cloth. The first one received mortar shrapnel in the abdomen, legs, and shoulders, in Brazil Street in Insha'at, four days ago. He was operated on at the national hospital and then transferred here. The second one took sniper bullets in the chest and arm, this morning, as he was buying bread, also in Brazil Street. He was operated on in another clandestine center in Baba 'Amr.

While I visit the wounded, Ra'id and Abu Bari continue to argue in the hallway. Then finally Abu Bari joins me and uncovers the girl, who was just next to me, hidden under a blanket. She wears a black scarf and a long blue dress. Ra'id

and I get permission to speak with her alone, without witnesses to influence her, in the pharmacy.

*This woman's story turned out to be completely incoherent,
which no doubt explains why the other journalists who collected her testimony couldn't use it. Her use of a very
dialectical Arabic didn't make the interview any easier. There
is certainly a basis of truth in this story, for several other
people told us about it, and confirmed the name of the*
mukhabarat *non-commissioned officer responsible, a certain
Abu 'Ali Mundhir. The woman also gave us the names of
young women kidnapped and raped by Mundhir; we tried to
find them, but in vain, and I don't see any sense in writing
their names down here, or the name of our witness. Here's
what we could gather from her story, which she told with a sly
little smile, throwing us flirting, sideways, coquettish glances
under her scarf. She comes from a little village on the road to
Palmyra, and she is illiterate, since where she comes from
girls don't learn how to read. At the age of fifteen, she got
married and came to live in Homs. Two years ago, she got
divorced, that's when she began working as an "artist," as
they say, in Hama and in her home town. Here, the story
loses all consistency: denunciation by the husband, arrest,
torture, medical examinations, no need to go into details.*

*It's in prison that she supposedly met Mundhir, a prison
guard. When she was freed, she returned to her village, then
two months later returned to Homs. Mundhir then supposedly
re-contacted her on her cellphone. He asked her to serve as bait
to capture two young sisters he wanted to exchange for some
young Alawite men detained by the FSA. The details of the
kidnapping aren't really of interest. The girl says she wasn't*

present at the rapes, but a woman from Aleppo who saw everything told her about them.

In the first room, near the entrance, two wounded have just arrived. We try to go in but some men refuse to let us see them: "There are rules." *Mukhabarat* reflexes? Paranoia is keen. They throw us out. "I don't want to see my photo on the TV!" shouts a young man who joins us near the car, with a smile. To see these wounded we need the permission of the military commander. Arguments start up again, it's endless. Abu Khattab, one of the doctors, finally explains to us that they're captured soldiers. "When it's us, the regime kills us! Whereas we take care of our prisoners!" – "Precisely," replies Ra'id, "so show them to us!" Impossible, we need permission from the Military Council. When Ra'id snaps at Abu Khattab, "Your methods are the regime's methods!" he is very upset. The situation is tense, there's a lot of shouting.

Afterward, Imad brings us to another medical center, smaller than Abu Bari's, but clean and orderly, set up in an apartment. No doctors, just two male nurses. They just have a few surgical supplies and can only carry out first aid. If it's a serious wound, they have to refer the patient else-where. Abu Bari's center is of the same level. Now, they are in the process of setting up a small clinic for Baba 'Amr, better equipped, capable of performing operations.

We would visit this new clinic a few days later. In my notes, the three clinics remain numbered in the order in which we visited them: the first is Abu Bari's medical center, the second this one, opened as we will learn by Imad and his friends, and the third is the clinic properly speaking, also set up by Imad's group with the support of the FSA.

———

10:20 AM. Return to Hassan's apartment. The men are seated around the stove and recounting their exploits. I drink whiskey, and it doesn't seem to bother anyone. The mood is much calmer than at Abu Bari's clinic. Ra'id explains that the activists have created an Information Bureau, and that all the journalists have to go through it, through this Jeddi he had got so angry with earlier. The line of the Bureau is clear, you can photograph anything peaceful – demonstrations, humanitarian aid, suffering of civilians and so on – but much less anything military, the FSA and its actions.

Bassam, one of the soldiers, tells us about an attack that took place three days ago. Some forty soldiers wanted to desert, but they were detained by the security forces who imprisoned them in what Bassam calls the "tower," a big building on Brazil Street. The soldiers, who were going to be executed, were held on the ninth floor; the security forces were entrenched on the eighth. Bassam, with two of his friends, attacked the tower with an RPG, firing three rockets at the eighth floor and killing some *mukhabarat*. Then they negotiated: release the deserters, or we kill you all. The forty men, along with two civilians, were allowed to leave.

Afterwards, Bassam recites a poem in classical Arabic. A wonderful music, rhythmic, emphatic, hammered out, beautiful to listen to even though I don't understand a word. Ra'id knew an officer who recited poems every day, they flowed from his mouth like water. But he is dead.

Bassam has a fine face, narrow, pointed, with a well-groomed beard and keen eyes, and a band around his slightly balding head. The face of a Chechen *boyevik* from the good old days. He is not a deserter, but a civilian who took up arms. Single, in his thirties, and he's not from here, he's from the countryside around Aleppo. Seeing the regime's crimes – the rapes, the murders, etc. – he decided a month ago to come from Aleppo to Baba 'Amr to join the FSA. He has a nephew who is at university here, who was part of the coordination committee of another city, and who introduced him to the FSA. Afterward, they saw how he behaved in combat.

Before, he was a journalist; magazines still solicit his work.

"Here, in Baba 'Amr, you're in a state within a state. It's the safest neighborhood in Syria. The people go out at night, they're not afraid of snipers. Al-Assad's tanks will pass over our bodies before they reach you.

"We fight for our religion, for our women, for our land, and lastly to save our skin. As for them, they're only fighting to save their skin."

He denies that the conflict, on their side, has a sectarian dimension: "We don't kill any human being on the basis of religion. 'He who kills a soul not in legitimate self-defense, it's as if he killed all of humanity,' says the Qur'an."

He talks to me about their organization. Baba 'Amr is commanded by a *Majlis al-'Askari*, a Military Council, headed by 'Abd ar-Razzaq Tlass and a dozen other officers.

Bassam is under their orders. The Council tries to inculcate a certain code of conduct, a certain ethos in the men. They come from the Army, where extreme practices were drilled into them: they're ready to do anything, to kill anyone. The Military Council tries to give them some moral training. In the Army, also, the soldiers are used to addressing people aggressively, rudely. The Military Council is trying to change these habits, so that the FSA soldiers have good relations with civilians. He gives me examples of correct behavior: when they capture officers, they don't mistreat them, but talk with them, and ask them, "Why are you killing us?"

Midnight. Ra'id shows his work, which seems to be received with appreciation. In the hallway, the soldiers are still dismantling, cleaning, oiling their weapons. Another Belgian 5.56 mm, handled by a chubby-faced soldier in a camouflage uniform with a beard and a white *keffiyeh* around his neck. These weapons are purchases, brought from Lebanon.

They teach me a phrase: *Ash-sha'ab yurid isqat an-nizam*, "The people want the fall of the regime."

Before we go to bed, one of the young men runs a vacuum cleaner through the room. Touching thoughtfulness.

It's funny, after so many years, to sleep again in a room full of young fighters and Kalashnikovs.

Friday, January 20

Baba 'Amr

Dream: my friend E. contacts me, panicking. He's going to prison for marijuana possession. He is very afraid of withdrawal symptoms. Then he's in a cell. Desperate. He has a neighbor whose anus is positioned in the middle of his back, and who can only shit lying on his side next to a Turkish toilet: "The poor guy. Some people have no luck." Visit with a kind of social worker. Long endless tirade by E., who talks about his misfortunes. I listen distractedly and begin reading. All of a sudden I realize he's sobbing furiously. "All this is because I had no father," he cries. "It's too hard for a child to grow up without a father." He stamps his feet, his face screwed up, I look at him finally and realize he's a little blond boy, lost in his fit of tears and anguish. He looks like my son Emir. I open my arms, he comes, and I hold him against me as he sobs uncontrollably.

Breakfast: omelet, tomatoes, *za'atar*, *labneh*, olives, cheeses.
   A young guy enters, we introduce ourselves, and right away he wants to tell a story: he has a friend who did three

months in jail because of a dream. He had dreamed that he was leading the President's motorcade; he told it to some friends, a stoolie denounced him, and he was arrested.

Everyone here has a story, and as soon as they see a foreigner they want to tell it to him.

Imad took a bullet through the left ankle, by ricochet, during an Army attack, in October not long before the 'Eid al-Adha. The bullet went through the joint, and he couldn't go to a clinic. He was taken care of by a pharmacist, it didn't heal well, it still hurts and he limps.

Magnificent sunny day. From the top of the building, a view of the roofs of Baba 'Amr, many unfinished constructions, but sometimes already partially inhabited as everywhere in Syria. Toward the northeast, beyond the Al-Bassel stadium, some residential towers, one of them still under construction, where Army snipers are hiding. Then the orchards, the immense chemical factory and the lake, invisible. Homs' center is on the other side, also invisible from here.

10:30 AM. Visit of Haqura with Imad. Deserted indeed beneath the cold sun, not a single inhabitant, the streets empty, dead. Just from time to time an FSA soldier, AK or RPG on his shoulder. On the ground: bullets, casings, mortar splinters, garbage everywhere. Near the FSA HQ from yesterday, the streets are walled off by sandbags. A man has come to his place to get his things. He left four months ago, the children couldn't bear the shooting.

The outer edge of the neighborhood is totally destroyed. This zone was heavily bombed, especially in November; there are mortar craters everywhere on the ground. Hassan's house, completely ravaged. I photograph Hassan in front of the ruins, from behind with his baby on his shoulder. Some corners are dangerous, open to sniper fire, we pass quickly hugging the walls. A little further on we enter another destroyed house. On the ground scattered anti-aircraft rounds, the tail of a mortar shell, Russian made, 82 mm. Through a shattered window, we can see an Army post 50 meters away. You have to look furtively, these guys shoot. Abu Yazan, one of the soldiers, holds his pistol cocked. Hassan is still walking his baby.

House. Holes in the walls, staircases. Through one window, you can see the post clearly, a little base in fact, a three-story building with a destroyed truck parked just next to it and balconies covered with sandbags riddled with holes. Here too you have to look quickly, stealthily. The post seems deserted but Abu Yazan is nervous. Behind are the stadium and the residential towers.

Like everywhere in the world, cats have left their paw prints in the concrete.

In an abandoned apartment, fragments of a doll, dishes, an ultrasound scan still in its envelope, made probably in Lebanon.

Another destroyed apartment, burned, riddled with bullet holes. In one completely burned room, a melted TV. On a bed, a cemetery of computers. A man on sentry duty, sitting on an office chair, Kalashnikov in hand, observes the Army positions through a shell hole in the wall.

We pass on the other side of the buildings, toward the frontline but in a corner of the street protected by another building. The façade of the apartments where we just were, above us, are riddled with mortar shell or rocket impacts. On the ground floor, a big abandoned gym, with pink walls and a gray marble floor, the machines covered with plaster, dominated by a long mirror pierced by an explosive round. In one corner, a big punching bag is slowly swinging.

———

12:30 PM. Friday demonstration. It begins at the neighborhood mosque. The men pray; in front, dozens of children chant slogans. Activists arrive with flags and posters. At the end of prayer, the men shout the *takbir* and pour in waves out of the mosque chanting *Allahu Akbar*! The procession forms quickly and heads toward the main street of Baba 'Amr. At the intersections, FSA soldiers keep watch; at the end of the avenue there is an Army position. The procession heads up the avenue waving flags, photos of *shahids*, signs, some slogans are in English ("WE WANT INTERNATIONAL PROTECTION"). Men, young and old, children, even babies with their fathers. But only men: the women watch from balconies or from the sidewalk. The procession passes under the sniper tower, without incident, then in front of a big mosque, the main one of Baba 'Amr I think, and a school, and finally turns right. More marked FSA presence, there is a post and quite a few armed men. We join the other processions of Baba 'Amr in the middle of a wide street for a monster demonstration: thousands of men chant the slogans, dance in rows, and shout the *takbir*; then comes the music, drums too, with dancing in a circle around them, the young people also continue to dance the *dhikr* in rows, crying out slogans. In the center of the demonstration, a large human oval forms around two activists perched on a ladder with microphones, starting up the slogans. Around them there are drums and the first dancers, signs in English addressed to the Arab League; all along one side the women stay grouped, a wall of white, pale pink, or black scarves. Many of them are carrying babies and heart-shaped balloons. They applaud with enthusiasm, shout, yodel, and also chant slogans. Men wave their shoes. The roofs and balconies are packed. On one of them, activists are filming. All this in a mood of mad, electric exhilaration, the people are hyped up, a level of joyful and desperate energy I have never seen before.

This Friday is dedicated "to the political prisoners."

Meeting by chance with G., a sympathetic Franco-Syrian gentleman, who is from Insha'at but has lived in Montpellier for fifteen years. He is leaving in two or three days, his wife can't take it anymore. "If they didn't shoot at the demonstrators, all of Homs would be out in the streets." He explains to me that the leader of the demonstration is a university student, in his third year of studying to be an engineer.

The demonstration drummer is a gypsy. Here, as elsewhere, they are often musicians.

I find Ra'id in the street, caught up in an altercation with Abu Hanin, one of the leaders of the Information Bureau. Abu

Hanin is berating us for not wanting to work with them; Ra'id
explains that we're going to finish with the FSA first, then we'll
be glad to come see them. G. gets a little involved, translates,
comments.

End of the demonstration. The people disperse. Volleys on
the main street, just as people are leaving. Women are running. The shots come from the east, from a bridge that
leads to the Alawite quarter. The avenue separates Baba
'Amr from Insha'at. A month ago, crossing this avenue was
very risky. But since the other checkpoint to the west was
evacuated, three weeks ago, it's been calmer.

––––––

After the demonstration, we ask Imad if we can meet 'Abd
ar-Razzaq Tlass, one of the main military leaders of Homs.
G., the Franco-Syrian gentleman, agrees to accompany us to
serve as my translator. We find Tlass at home, on the first try.

2:00 PM. 'Abd ar-Razzaq Tlass, leader of the Military
Council of Baba 'Amr. Young guy, bearded, in a tracksuit.
He receives us in a room on the ground floor of a building,
with some AKs in a corner and a flag of the *katiba* al-Faruk
on the wall. He doesn't want to give an interview: it's out
of principle, their own journalists are enough. He is also
paranoid because foreign journalists, according to him,
have deformed his statements because of a pro-regime
bias. Ra'id tries to convince him, I argue too with the help
of G. who has kindly accompanied us. Tlass, politely: "We
have doubts about interviews. The situation is tense. We
don't trust foreign journalists." He doesn't want to talk

about military matters. "Your presence here poses problems for us."

Imad: "They have internal difficulties specific to them,
they don't want to talk about them."

Tlass: "The period when we showed things is over. If
your peoples haven't understood for eleven months, there's
no point." Conclusion: "*Bukra, insha'Allah.*"[28]

Disjointed conversation. I try 'Abd ar-Razzaq Tlass
again: Would he at least agree to talk about his own personal journey? Yes, he agrees. He is twenty-six, and comes
from Rastan. He was *mulazim awwal* in the 5th Division,
infantry, posted in Dara'a. His colleagues took part in the
repression, but he refused, and around February–March
obtained a change of post. He then began to take part in the
demonstrations, in civilian clothes, leaving the camp. He
mentions several massacres of demonstrators, including
one on February 24 in Sanzamin, which he did not witness
himself; same for a demonstration in Anchel, end of
February, after which he received a call to give blood, for
the wounded. These demonstrations were suppressed by
the 9th Division, the military *mukhabarat*, and State
Security. 'Abd ar-Razzaq Tlass was very disturbed by all
these wounded, by the difficulties in caring for them, by the
massacres. He never believed the regime's propaganda. "In
principle the Army should be neutral. It should protect
the people, the Nation. And there, we saw the opposite. The
checkpoints shot at people. Dara'a was devastated.
The people try to convince the Army to join them, against
the *mukhabarat*. But it didn't work. Because the officers

---

28 "Tomorrow, God willing."

gave the order to attack. They're allies of al-Assad, of the regime. The majority were Alawite. As for the Sunnis, they obey or they go to jail."

When he first thought about deserting, he wanted to do it in a group. With other officers, he tried to organize the mutiny of two *liwas* and one *katiba*[29] belonging to the 5th, 9th, and 15th Divisions. But finally the other officers took fright, because of the Air Force, and backed down. So he left alone, with his weapon. "I'm the first officer to have deserted the Syrian Army. Many people have tried to convince me not to do it: 'How can you do that, how can you even imagine that, deserting?'"

"I deserted in June, in Dara'a. I did it so as not to shoot at people, and I immediately took up arms. I saw you can't take down this regime without arms. I came to Rastan, where the Army was attacking, and I founded the Khalid ibn Walid *katiba*." Tlass formed the *katiba* with seven officers and about forty non-commissioned officers. When it was operational, he left it in the hands of other officers and came, around the second week of July, to form the al-Faruk *katiba*, here in Baba 'Amr. In August, it in turn was operational.

'Abd ar-Razzaq Tlass, here, presents the facts in his manner. The later defection of officers of higher rank than the subordinate officers who had first deserted and formed the first katibas *of the Free Army caused strong tensions, with the superior officers claiming that they should now take over*

---

29   A *liwa* is a brigade, a *katiba* is a battalion. 'Abd ar-Razzaq Tlass and his colleagues, then, were planning the mutiny of between 10,000 and 12,000 men.

command, something the subordinate officers who had been commanding for months accepted with difficulty. 'Abd ar-Razzaq Tlass had in fact been pushed out of the Khalid ibn Walid katiba *for such reasons. An ambitious man, he also attributes to himself a leading role in the al-Faruk* katiba, *which other interlocutors contest.*

The current leader of the Khalid ibn Walid *katiba* is the *raid*[30] Ahmad Bahbuh.

'Abd ar-Razzaq Tlass thinks that the number of soldiers would justify al-Faruk being a *liwa*, but they don't want to change the name. He thinks the Khalid ibn Walid *katiba* has over 4,000 or 5,000 men, which would also make it a *liwa*.

The al-Faruk *katiba* is responsible for the city of Homs, Telbisi, and the al-Qusayr zone. The Khalid ibn Walid *katiba* controls Rastan and the villages around it.

The al-Faruk *katiba* is commanded by a Military Council, but 'Abd ar-Razzaq Tlass has the final decision.

I ask him a question about his relations with Colonel Riad al-Asa'ad [*the commander of the Free Syrian Army, based in Antioch, Turkey*]: "For now, I can't answer that."

A freer discussion with Imad. They tell us the story of the Army base we saw this morning, with the burned truck next to it. The FSA had in fact captured the captain in charge of it. But they got along well with him, and they freed him provided he evacuate the position. Which he did,

---

30   Major.

withdrawing to the towers further back. Now he is observing a truce with the FSA.

'Abd ar-Razzaq Tlass tells us about the visit of the observers from the Arab League. They came, but on the other side of the big avenue. In the beginning, they didn't dare cross it, because of the shooting; then, two days later, they crossed over, five or eight of them, without handlers. At that time – it was the first week of the observers' mission [*toward the end of December 2011*] – the neighborhood was surrounded, under pressure. The observers came to convince them to negotiate with the Army. The FSA replied: "You're here to observe and report on what the Army is doing to us!" In fact the observers wanted to negotiate full respect for the agreement [*by the Syrian government*] in exchange for a retreat of the FSA.

Lunch with 'Abd ar-Razzaq Tlass. Scrambled eggs, eggs with meat, hummus, tomatoes, *za'atar*. The bread is heated by placing it on top of the *sobia*, or by sticking it on the side.

At one point, G. receives a phone call from his wife, who orders him to come home. He leaves us, apologizing, and it's once again Ra'id who will finish translating the discussion.

We try to convince 'Abd ar-Razzaq Tlass to show us the wounded soldiers from yesterday [*the ones at Abu Bari's clinic*]. First he talks about an informer, an Alawite *shabbiha* who gave information on the FSA's weapons caches. Then we're told they have a secret prison that they don't want to show to us. The soldiers are there too.

Me: "It's important that you show the world that you are decent people, patriots, that you treat wounded enemies well. That you're not Al-Qaʿida."

ʿAbd ar-Razzaq Tlass: "If this continues, we'll become just like Al-Qaʿida. If the world abandons us, and supports al-Assad, we will attack Israel and other countries, internationalize the conflict, to force the international community to intervene. We'll declare jihad." He asserts that these are not his personal views, that the Military Council of Homs has discussed it and that they all agree.

He wants a NATO military intervention. "If there's no NATO intervention, we'll call for jihad in the entire Muslim world. Then, groups will come from all over the Muslim world. And it will be war against *kufr* [*impiety*], and so it won't be limited to the Syrian question. Things will be out of our hands. And the struggle against Israel will resume."

ʿAbd ar-Razzaq Tlass explains that the idea is to put pressure on the West, so that the West will intervene before it becomes a regional war.

It's a very naïve vision, of course. He thinks that they can force Europe and the United States to intervene. They are all convinced that the United States is keeping al-Assad in power in order to support Israel. They hope to force their hand by threatening to provoke regional chaos.

"We tried everything and nothing works. This Friday we called 'the Friday before the declaration of jihad.' It's been two months since we've been trying to delay the call for jihad, but a majority voted in favor. We're at the service of the people, we have to follow suit."

At the demonstration, as noted above, they had told me that this Friday had been named for "the political prisoners." This system of naming the days, especially Fridays, is done on various forums, on Facebook or other websites, on the basis of votes by internet users. Apparently there are competing websites, hence the discrepancy between the two "names" for this Friday. The low number of voters means this is not very representative of the public opinion of Syria in revolt.

'Abd ar-Razzaq Tlass insists, referring to the fact that the demonstrators today were crying out: "*Labayk, labayk, labayk ya'Allah!*" This is a ritual phrase for arriving in Mecca, which means, "God, here I am!" (*Labayk* means: "We submit to you.") So this signifies that they're ready to go to their death, that they're ready for jihad.

When we leave, 'Abd ar-Razzaq Tlass accompanies us with a singsong: "God, let us go to jihad." Big laughter on all sides.

In the street, before we separate, we again ask him the question about his relations with Riad al-Asa'ad: "The FSA, it's inside [*the country*], that's all." He means: we don't have to take orders from the outside. "He and I, we take our orders from the people. If you want to go against them, you're traitors." On the question of the declaration of jihad, he doesn't know Riad's opinion. They have big communication problems.

Another important point not mentioned during this conversation is the fact that Tlass is a distant relative of Mustafa Tlass, the all-powerful Minister of Defense and right-hand man, for thirty years, of Hafez al-Assad. Even though Tlass has been in retirement since 2006, his extended family, present at every level in the Army, remains one of the most powerful Sunni clans in the country, and the defection of one of its members represents a major step for the regime. The television network Al-Dunya announced the death of 'Abd ar-Razzaq Tlass on February 9, but the FSA never confirmed it.

———

Not many people at nightfall. Freezing cold. Aside from a few avenues, the buildings huddle very close together, barely enough room for two cars to pass each other, no sidewalks. Oppressive feeling when you drive around these streets, like at the bottom of a narrow canyon, weaving between parked cars, motorbikes, and people.

———

4:30 PM. Muhammad Abu Sayyef, humanitarian coordinator for Baba 'Amr. An out-of-work electrical engineer, who volunteered to draw up lists of needy families and coordinate the distribution of aid. Salt-and-pepper beard cut short, fingerless gloves, white wool cap, white and gray tracksuit under a black leather jacket.

He explains: rise of the dollar, 30 per cent; rise in the price of essential goods, 20 per cent, because it's dangerous to bring them to the neighborhood. Thus total rise of prices: 50 per cent. Previously, the factories delivered their products. Now, wholesalers and semi-wholesalers have to go find them themselves.

Example of a canister of cooking gas. The normal price is 250 Syrian pounds [*US $3.47 at the current rate*]. That's still the price in Zahra, Akrama, and Nezha (pro-regime neighborhoods). But there's no more state distribution in Baba 'Amr. Private individuals bring the canisters into the neighborhood at their own risk. So the price in Baba 'Amr varies between 500 and 900 SYP per bottle [*between US $6.90 and US $12.40*].

A man named 'Abdelkafi L., a friend of Imad, was recently killed for gas. Ten days ago, he left to get some canisters for resale in a border zone between pro- and anti-regime neighborhoods. There, you can find gas at a higher price than the official price, but less than in Baba 'Amr, so he could eke out a profit. There were two of them in the car, a little Suzuki van, but in these zones there's shooting: 'Abdelkafi was wounded in the leg and arrested; his friend managed to escape. 'Abdelkafi was taken to the military hospital – the FSA got the information through nurse sympathizers, sent to find out. Three days ago, they received his body, with traces of torture all over it, by electricity etc. On the face of it he was killed at the military hospital. The case is documented, the corpse was shown on Al Jazeera.

When someone is kidnapped or arrested, they pay to find out where he is, and sometimes to recover the body.

———

Return to the first clinic. We're not allowed to enter. Violent shouting match between Ra'id and Abu Bari, the fat bearded pseudo-mujahideen, arrogant and stupid. "I don't give a flying fuck about 'Abd ar-Razzaq Tlass! [*Yesterday he said the opposite.*] He's a soldier, we're civilians. I'm so furious I hate everyone!" Imad doesn't know who put him in charge of the clinic. He's a former plasterer, without any medical training whatsoever.

It's Imad who created the second clinic we saw, in the apartment, because he was fed up with the way the first one was managed. He wants a clinic under the control of doctors.

We learn that it's Abu Bari who set up the first clinic, and he's the one who had the doctors come. That's why he can keep control of the place.

————

5:30 PM. After the evening demonstration, we are summoned by the Military Council. The guys who came to get us are nervous, and the tension quickly rises. Ra'id is afraid they're going to erase his photos. As a precaution, I send a text message to *Le Monde* to warn them. But in fact it's just to get to know us, a very cordial meeting in a room to the back of a school. Fifteen men are seated against the walls; an officer leads the discussion, someone whom Ra'id has already met during the noon demonstration. His name is Muhannad al-'Umar. A calm, serious, intelligent man. Imad briefs him on the problem with Abu Bari's clinic, and Muhannad says he'll settle it. Then he asks a first question: what does the French government think of the death of Gilles Jacquier? We explain the declarations, more or less suspicious of the regime, of Alain Juppé. Then we ask their opinion. It's the *mukhabarat*, they reply. But they don't think the journalists were targeted: for them, the *mukhabarat* were targeting the pro-Assad demonstration, so that the journalists would film this massacre and thus give credit to the official argument about terrorism.

Then Ra'id asks for specific permissions: free access to Abu Bari's clinic, and to the prisoners.

The wounded soldier is apparently a non-commissioned officer in the *mukhabarat*. They agree for us to see him, and accept that it be one-on-one so we can be assured he isn't being pressured.

Muhannad al-'Umar is a civilian who joined the FSA. He takes part in military actions and does logistical support. He is a member of the *Majlis al-'Askari*, the Military Council. There aren't many civilians in the Council, just three members out of a total of twenty-four. The Council heads the entire al-Faruk *katiba*, over all its zone of operation – Homs, al-Qusayr, etc. Muhannad doesn't want to say how many men they have. He is already wanted by the *mukhabarat*, that's why he has no problem with us taking down or publishing his name. Again he strikes me with his calm, reasonable, sensible, poised bearing.

———

Return by car with Imad to the apartment of Hassan's men. Quick burst of acceleration at an intersection, because of the snipers.

9:45 PM. Seven months ago, Imad tells us, he and his friends burned down a beer shop. The owner was Alawite, he was photographing the demonstrations and the FSA accused him of transmitting information to the *mukhabarat*.

Saturday, January 21

Baba 'Amr

As on every night, long, dense dreams, endless, very structured. In front of my house, the Castellaras terrace; the big pot of strawberries is still there, I water them but they're no good, tasteless, impossible to eat; however, there's a new branch, raspberries, red and fleshy; I pick them one by one, there are four of them, and I have no intention of sharing. Afterward, it continues, in various spaces.

———

Al-Maktab al-I'ilami, the Information Bureau. Jeddi is one of the people in charge. They control the information in Baba 'Amr, and have insisted since the beginning on supervising us, on supervising all journalists; in principle, they control journalists' access to Baba 'Amr, and within the neighborhood access to strategic places, like demonstrations or the clinic. Thanks to Ra'id's contacts, we came in with the FSA, avoiding them; since his altercation with Jeddi, then yesterday at the demonstration with Abu Hanin, we have cut loose from them and remain with the FSA. This creates tensions, but it's much better for us. We'll go and see them at the end, when we've done everything that interests us. With them, we'd see only what they want us to see, and they'd be acting as if the FSA didn't exist, a rather basic and unsophisticated control of discourse, worthy of the *mukhabarat* whose methods they have absorbed since childhood. As G. said yesterday at the demonstration, during the altercation with Abu Hanin, in his so pleasant French: "*Il faut les comprendre, monsieur. Quarante ans de peur!*"[31] But before killing the real Bashar, they'll have to kill the Bashar in their heads.

The Information Bureau seemed to be afraid that images of the FSA might serve the regime's propaganda, by giving plausibility to the argument that the government is fighting terrorists. At the time of our visit, it was still difficult to make them understand that they couldn't simply deny the armed dimension of the uprising. The FSA, on its side, let us freely observe and photograph its weapons, its men, and its fighting. It should be added that after the beginning of the massive bombing of Homs, on February 3, these nuances lost all importance.

12:45 PM. Excursion. Visit to the command post of Hassan, who promises me a translator. Then we head off with Imad to a commercial street beyond the central avenue, quite animated, with taxis, shops. It's the old Baba 'Amr.

An elderly gentleman on a bike: "It's gotten much better here." We discuss the prisoner releases Bashar al-Assad promised to the Arab League. Another gentleman, Abu 'Adil, explains that his fifty-year-old brother has been

31   "You have to understand them, Monsieur. Forty years of fear!"

detained for three months. Three people arrested with him were returned dead. He wasn't freed but transferred to Damascus, to a secret prison. "He was arrested at home, for nothing. Here, in Syria, you mustn't ask why."

We pick up my young translator, Adam, an FSA guy. His English is limited but it will do. Further on, at an intersection, an FSA checkpoint controls the traffic, sometimes checks the drivers. Discussion. With several soldiers, in a room, we look at maps on Ra'id's computer, and they explain to me where the Army positions are. A big explosion outside, a mortar, followed by gunfire, the checkpoint further up opening fire.

A young soldier from the checkpoint, Fadi, is an Alawite. Adam translates as well as he can. Fadi is from Jiblaya, a village near Tartus. He joined the FSA in July or August, in Homs. Because he saw the Army killing civilians, he said to himself: "I am not with them, I am with these people. It is not: I am Alawi, so I am with Alawi. No. If they do wrong, I try to do right."

In the street, the shooting continues.

Fadi was *mulaẓim awwal*. One of his friends, a Sunni *mulaẓim awwal* named 'Ali, refused an order to kill civilians, in Kfar 'Aaya, and they shot him in the back. He survived, but remained paralyzed. Fadi deserted two weeks later. He didn't announce his desertion, to protect his family. Only his brother knows; in the beginning, he was against it, but ended up accepting it. I ask: "How did the FSA accept you, without taking you for a spy or an agent provocateur?" He already had a friend in the FSA, who vouched for him. "Now I am very happy, not like before. When you are in the Army, if you know a big man, you live well. If you don't, you are shit."

Here in Baba 'Amr, there are five or six Alawites in the FSA. He has no problem. "I never heard: We want to kill Alawis. Only specific people who have committed crimes." Alawites take women hostage, and this makes him sick. Recently, the FSA captured an Alawite he knew; he hadn't done anything bad, so they let him go. First they tried to exchange him, but the other side refused, and they let him go all the same: "I was very pleased to see this."

We leave. The bullets continue to resound. The street where we are is safe, but further on it's open.

————

Visit with Imad to a neighborhood next to the railroad, behind the Hamzi mosque. Many destroyed buildings. We climb to the fourth floor with some inhabitants, in an apartment riddled with bullets and BTR ammunition, 14.5 mm. The kitchen wall is full of holes. The owner, Abu 'Abdu, built another wall, inside, to make a room, but they shot through that too. Some shots even passed through three walls and ended up in his neighbor's apartment. Abu 'Abdu brought his wife and children to her family, but there are too many other women there, no room, he can't stay there. He's thinking of rebuilding the wall a second time and reinforcing it with sandbags, to be able to live there.

Through the holes and a window, we see the post, blue sandbags arranged around a passage over the elevated railroad. It's the checkpoint of the Kfar 'Aaya intersection. A pickup leaves and moves off. I photograph it discreetly through a shell hole, zooming in. In the photo you also see a tank turret, seemingly covered with blue plastic, its cannon pointed straight at us.

In the street with the inhabitants. Devastated neighborhood, all the houses facing the checkpoint are riddled with impacts by large-caliber weapons and bombs. They show me the remains of a shell, a kind of cluster bomb.

Seven dead in the immediate neighborhood, sixteen people arrested. The soldiers come from the checkpoint, break down the doors, and arrest people. Not many FSA here, they can't stop them.

This area has been calm for two Fridays, since around January 6, the time when the Arab League observers came to Homs. But twenty days ago there were three very deadly days: the first day, eighteen dead, the second, nine dead, the third, seven dead. Shooting at the funerals caused many wounded. A man shows me the scar from the bullet that passed through his leg.

Two FSA soldiers arrive on motorbike. Recent deserters. They show their Army cards and pose proudly with them, their faces uncovered.

It's hard for the FSA to take up positions here because of the towers [of the university], which dominate the neighborhood, and of the snipers. They come in force only when there's a fight. The towers are impregnable, protected by BRDMs and 200 soldiers who defend the snipers on the upper floors.

Hamzi mosque. Brand-new, still incomplete and not yet consecrated. Riddled with bullet holes, a few shells, the windows shattered. View through it to the towers. We enter from the back by going over the wall, under the eyes of possible snipers, a slightly uncomfortable situation. But nothing happens. The inside is vast and bare, almost complete, but not quite. We step on broken glass. We climb to the roof, around the cupola: we don't go to the side where the towers are, no reason to tempt the devil.

In the car, discussion with Imad about access to the clinic [*of Abu Bari*]. Imad doesn't want any problems. We have to have Abu Khattab's permission to enter.

———

Return to the Military Council. A man talks: his niece S. Sh., twenty-two years old, a student of Arabic literature and a hair stylist, was kidnapped by security forces four and a half months ago, in August. She was returning to her hair salon in Insha'at, near the Quba' mosque. There was no reason to arrest her, she hadn't done anything; she was taken at eight in the morning, long before the demonstration. People who were set free saw her and told them she was with the Air Force *mukhabarat*, which the '*amid*,[32] when the shaykhs went to see him, as they do for all the kidnapped women, confirmed. The '*amid* of the Air Force *mukhabarat* is named Jawdad, he's Druze. As for the general who commands Homs, he's an Alawite named Yusef Wannus.

---

32 Brigadier general.

As we talk, volleys of gunfire. It's the checkpoint we saw, the one in Kfar 'Aaya, which is firing.

Big discussion: the officers know girls who have been abused, raped, but the social rules mean that the families will never let us talk to them. The shame is too great. Ra'id tries to convince them, once again.

We're summoned to see the funeral of a *shahid*. During the time it takes us to reach the mosque, the funeral has already left. We are told he was killed by the volleys we heard, but that seems hard to believe.

———

Imad takes us to his clinic. The two prisoners are there, lying under blankets. A doctor is tending to the first one's ankle, pierced by a bullet. The other is wounded in the hand. They are young, thinly bearded, Sunnis from Idlib. The one wounded in the hand is named Ahmad H. and is twenty. He tells us: They had come to Baba 'Amr in a military ambulance to recover a wounded soldier, on Friday the 13th. Their own comrades, from the tower on Brazil Street, shot at them before they could reach the wounded man. So they turned back and came to Baba 'Amr. As soon as they're better, they'll join the FSA.

The doctors change the bandages. Ahmad has lost the little finger of his right hand. Bears the procedure stoically, barely grimaces.

The art of taking decent pictures without a single face.

After the treatment, we find ourselves in the office with Imad and the doctor. The doctor explains why he doesn't want to work at the other health center: it's impossible because of Abu Bari's monopoly. Doctors have no say, including Abu Khattab. We decide to go back to see the situation, after the promises [*of Muhannad al-'Umar*].

Short walk from Imad's clinic to Abu Bari's, still with Adam. At one street corner we eat *ful* with our fingers from little bowls, standing in front of the street peddler's cart. Ra'id goes to buy some *sfihas* with meat and cheese, we also drink the *ful* juice like soup. At the end of the avenue, the sun is setting, tinting the surrounding grays with orange. A few shots still ring out.

5:30 PM. Arrival at the clinic. Another violent shouting match between Ra'id and Abu Bari, who categorically refuses us access. He tells his friends that the Military Council has forbidden our entry. Ra'id calls Muhannad, then passes him to Abu Bari; Abu Bari hangs up without handing the phone back and says that Muhannad confirms. "The *Majlis al-'Askari* and Muhannad forbid you." The tone rises. Ra'id: "You're fighting against Bashar to replace him with the same authoritarianism. Here you're the one controlling everything, deciding everything, the doctors shut their traps; you decide everything against the opinion of the Military Council, against the opinion of the doctors." – "Since we're worse than the regime, you won't go in." A shift to threats. "If you stay here, you'll see things you don't want to." – "Are you threatening me?" – "Yes, I'm threatening you." So we go a little further away to wait for Imad, who comes to get us in his car.

6:00 PM. Imad takes us to the third clinic, the real one, where they're setting up an operating room in case of a blockade of Baba 'Amr.

Al-Muthanna, a pharmacist, knows Ra'id from his last visit. [*He insists, like all his colleagues, on the question of danger for the medical staff.*] "It's very dangerous to be a doctor or a pharmacist in Baba 'Amr. If we leave the neighborhood, they can arrest us and detain us for three to six months, just to prevent us from working." Three doctors from Baba 'Amr have been arrested, along with two pharmacists and some nurses. Most of them have recently been freed. One of the pharmacists, Jamal F., was killed during his detention, four months ago.

Gestures: "They look at your papers, they see: Baba 'Amr, and they arrest you." Al-Muthanna hasn't left the neighborhood for six months.

Abu Ibrahim comes in, a nurse who was imprisoned in September. He worked at the National Hospital. Denounced for treating revolutionaries and arrested. Mimes the scene with big gestures, recounting: beaten with clubs, his eyes blindfolded, "You, come here!" Hard slaps. He was whipped with a thick rubber cable and given electric shocks. He shows us the scars from the blows on his legs. The wounds got infected, as there was no hygiene, no shower.

He was arrested by the Army, after that he doesn't know where he was transferred as his eyes were blindfolded. (Fears he might be identified, doesn't want to give details.)

But says his treatment was relatively OK. He was enti-
tled to special treatment because he's a nurse: they didn't
break his bones. Afterwards, he was able to take care of
other prisoners.

Detail of the tortures: on the first day, he was mistreated for
nine hours. Then after four days, mistreated again. This is
due to the rotation of the interrogators. He was interrogated
three times in twelve days, mistreated each time. Hung on the
wall by one wrist, with a plastic cord, on tiptoe, for four to five
hours: *ash-Shabah*, a specific method. He mimes the position.

He stayed in prison for a month. Released because they
didn't find anything and couldn't prove anything; he denied
everything, and they ended up letting him go.

Two other men in the room. Abu Abdallah, a military
doctor who hasn't returned to work since the end of
December, and Abu Salim, a doctor of the military
mukhabarat, who hasn't returned since November. It's Abu
Salim who heads this clinic. He thinks of himself as a
deserter, but hasn't announced it. He was born here, his
friends are here. Seeing the treatment inflicted on the neighborhood and the prisoners, he decided to join the people
and live with them, or else die with them.

He worked in Damascus, in five different services, then
in Latakia. He was with the *mukhabarat* for the past two
years, and saw how the situation evolved before and after
the revolution. He can testify to the tortures.

"What is the mission of a *mukhabarat* doctor? I'll explain
that to you.

"His first mission: keep people subjected to torture alive
so they can be tortured for as long as possible.

"The second: in case the person interrogated passes out, give him first aid so the interrogation can continue.

"The third: supervise the use of psychotropic drugs during interrogation. Chlorpromazine [*Thorazine or Megaphen*], Diazepam/Valium, Ketamine/Ketalar, and 90 degree alcohol, a liter in the nose or the eyes, or injected subcutaneously – alcohol is used to wake people up but also to torture.

"The fourth: if the person tortured has passed his threshold of resistance, the doctor brings him to the military hospital. Before the revolution, the patient was handcuffed behind his back; since the revolution, the patient has his eyes blindfolded and is handcuffed to the doctor. Before, all patients in danger of death were attended to; now, only the important prisoners; the others are left to die. The decision isn't in the doctor's hands: if he sees the prisoner is in danger of death, he sends a report to the one in charge, who decides and signs the transfer orders.

"At the hospital, the attending doctor can't talk to the patient; if he has a question, he must address the *mukhabarat* doctor, who asks the patient, then answers the doctor.

"Since the beginning of the revolution, if an important prisoner is brought to the military hospital – in some very specific cases – he is tied to the bed and two guards are posted in front of the door. Only the *mukhabarat* doctor or the head doctor of the hospital can administer treatment. Even the *mukhabarat* doctor is searched by the guards every time he leaves the room, to go to the bathroom for instance, and then again when he returns."

Long story of Abu Salim. In Damascus, in the Regional Section, there are Arabs detained since 1985. The two most dangerous ones are Lebanese; among the others, there are eleven Lebanese, two Jordanians, and one Algerian. They are incarcerated in very harsh conditions. At the end of 2010 they went on hunger strike with three demands:

- the right to read newspapers;
- the right to fresh bread;
- food that doesn't smell bad.

Abu Salim was sent by the man in charge to negotiate with them, supervised by two officers from Security who let him speak. The strike lasted for a month and three days; finally the *mukhabarat* agreed to the demands.

The two dangerous prisoners are imprisoned in a cell that measures 3 m by 1.6 m, with open toilets. At the door, there is a 20×30 cm hole. On top of the wall, a 50×30 cm opening. To open the window – if the temperature rises in summer for example – the doctor must write a report and obtain permission.

Abu Salim doesn't know why they are there. But one day he was handcuffed to one of them, returning from the hospital to a *mukhabarat* building, and when the guards couldn't find the key he found himself briefly alone with him: "What's the problem with you?" – "I had a problem with the big boss" (Hafez al-Assad).

The discussion continues at Abu Salim's place, in a freezing reception room. Abu Ibrahim, the nurse, brings some fuel oil and heats the place. Coffee, cigarettes.

Al-Muthanna, the pharmacist, wants our opinion: "What were the mistakes of the revolution? What should we have done differently?"

Me: "There haven't been any mistakes till now. You've taken the right path, chosen the right strategy. Pressure on the regime is increasing from day to day. The demonstrations are increasing, the desertions are increasing. The regime seems very solid to you, and that's normal, you're suffering, but it's a wooden house gnawed by termites: one day, you tap on the walls, and everything falls into dust. And you are the termites. The path is the right one, but it's long and there aren't any shortcuts. On the other hand, you should avoid the temptation to radicalization. The impatience of soldiers, the temptation of jihad. That can turn everything around. But the regime has already lost. It will never go back to the situation of before the revolution. Because the fear has been lifted, people are no longer afraid of the regime as they were before."

Question about France: what can they do for France to increase pressure on Russia? I explain that we'll have to wait for the end of the Arab League process. When it has obviously failed, the West can say: fine, the Arabs tried, that didn't work, now we'll move on to something else.

Ra'id translates and elaborates. He also explains the role of the UN Human Rights Commission, which is preparing a second report. The doctors, including Abu Salim, understand and suggest preparing a file, with all the names of those responsible for the repression they know, and proven facts.

They ask questions about the international protection of medical structures. Would like to join Doctors Without Borders. I explain it doesn't work like that. Protection is more the realm of the ICRC.[33] In principle, the Red Cross/ Red Crescent symbol protects a hospital. Attacking it is a war crime under international law. But here that would make it a target. One more war crime means nothing to the regime.

They tell us a story: before, wearing a beard was in itself a motive for indictment: "Ah, you're part of bin Laden's gang." Now, they arrest a student: "What are you studying?" – "French literature." – "Ah, you're part of the Sarkozy gang, *jama'at Sarkozy*!" It's a true story: "You can meet the student." He was kept in prison for twenty-one days, three months ago.

Al-Muthanna explains that marbles are forbidden, because they can serve as weapons against the Army, using slingshots. If they enter a house and find marbles, they arrest the father. So parents forbid their children from playing with them. One man from Baba 'Amr was arrested for that three days ago.

Abu Salim affirms that even children are under surveillance. They asked his son what channels his parents watch; he knew he had to be careful, so he answered well. But the parents of children who replied Al Jazeera, Al Arabiya, France 24, BBC, El-Wiral, 'Adnan al-'Arur (a Saudi preacher, anti-Syrian regime), etc. were summoned. In some schools, an armed guy from Security even handed out

---

33   International Committee of the Red Cross.

questionnaires to the children in ninth class – twelve-year-olds – about their parents' habits. The teachers are forced to accept.

Examples of questions: what channels do your parents watch? (They are listed.) Do your parents watch Dunya TV? How do they react during the President's speeches? Do your relatives take part in the demonstrations? Are there weapons at your house?

They tell us about the kidnappings. H.R., a woman kidnapped in Insha'at a month ago by the *shabbiha*, released after four days in an exchange, with two other girls, for pro-regime men kidnapped by the FSA. There is also the S. family in Insha'at, whose daughter H.S. was detained for five days. Abu Abdallah, the military doctor, knows her.

A little earlier, Abu Abdallah offered me a beautiful *misbaha*[34] made of little glass beads, in the colors of free Syria, made in prison by his brother.

'Ali, another doctor, shows us his torso, crisscrossed with scars. He caught several bullets on October 28, including one a centimeter away from his heart, and one 1.5 centimeters away from his spine. Some *shabbiha*, four men armed with Kalashnikovs and a machine gun, in a black KIA, entered the neighborhood, greeting the FSA people in a friendly way, and then machine-gunned the demonstration. Afterwards, they managed to flee through Kfar 'Aaya and rejoin the checkpoint. There were six dead, including a woman. Ra'id remembers, he had photographed the bodies

---

34 Prayer beads.

of the dead. 'Ali had already been announced as *shahid*, and they had begun digging his grave. "I'm the living martyr."

———

Just as we arrive at the house, gunfire breaks out, some nearby (outgoing fire apparently). Heavy exchanges. It resumes a little later, after a mortar detonation, then it's more and more sustained. It is 10:45 PM. We get dressed and go out, escorted by 'Alaa who is carrying an AK-74.[35] We go to Hassan's command post where a few guys, in the dark, with just the light of a cellphone, are trying to load an obviously jammed machine gun. We go further on, with another soldier, along the street of semi-destroyed buildings where we were yesterday. When we reach an intersection, with a street that looks out on to the Army positions, 'Alaa explains to us that we have to cross at a fast run. We run fast. At that moment the post begins firing, single shots then volleys. We continue, we look for Hassan. Then the other soldier calls him on the phone. He has left for Insha'at, where the main attack is taking place. Who attacked first? "We never attack," 'Alaa replies. "When the Army attacks, we defend ourselves." About-face, another crossing of the street at a run, then we calmly return to the house.

Surprising tranquility during the minutes spent waiting to contact Hassan, in the corner of a street in the dark. Gunfire on various sides, and us in the cold and the quiet, calm.

———

35 A more modern but less common version of the Kalashnikov.

Imad gives us another version of the story of the two prisoners we saw at the second clinic. The FSA had attacked an Army building, and the two soldiers fled; wounded, they were captured, and it's only at that point that they said: "We're with you." But the FSA considers them prisoners [*and not deserters*].

Army snipers have two functions: shooting at passersby, and at soldiers who try to desert. That's what happened with those two.

Fadi, Abu Yazan, and Hassan return from the fight. Fadi had tried to fire an RPG that Abu Yazan dismantles in front of us, but it misfired.

We give them a hard time because they didn't bring anything to eat.

Abu Yazan tells the story of the fight: there is an FSA checkpoint in Insha'at, in a school. The Army attacked and the guys called for reinforcements. They knew there was a sniper in the upper stories of the tower under construction near the tall blue building, and that's why they took RPGs, to dislodge him. Fired one. Even if they miss him – they shoot at random, not knowing what floor he's on – it's supposed to scare him and force him to come down.

12:45 AM. Dinner finally arrives. Imad yodels for joy, takes out his pistol and shoots a bullet through the window, howling with laughter. I scold him: "It's not polite to make holes in the walls and the windows, when you're a guest in someone's home."

Sunday, January 22

Baba 'Amr

Slow awakening. *Za'atar*, *labneh*, cheese.

The dreams keep proliferating, personal and disturbing.

Outside. Cold, fog. The neighborhood deserted in the mist. In front of the command post a few soldiers start trickling in, Muhammad Z. from the Military Council, on a motorbike, Abu Yazan a little later. Comparison of Russian and Chinese Kalashnikovs, jokes, laughter. The men practice their three words of English.

The FSA's weaponry is completely motley: Russian, Chinese, Czech, Belgian, American, Spanish, Italian . . .

Mohammed Z. takes us on his motorcycle toward the heart of Baba 'Amr, to a little street. Two women and a man come out of a house: the women lost their father there, when a mortar shell fell in front of the door. It happened at the end of December. The traces are still visible: torn metal of the doors, a felled electrical pole.

Inside an apartment, on a bed with blankets and an IV drip, a very thin man, emaciated but smiling, Z. He has lost his left leg, beneath the knee. The stump is still covered with an enormous bandage.

The room is full of people, an old woman, other women, children, many men, his brother. Everyone takes part in telling his story.

[*Z. had his leg half torn off by the same shell that killed the father of the two women I met in the street.*] His brother's son, 'Ali, had part of his arm cut off by the shrapnel; a neighboring woman was also wounded. All three were brought in vehicles to the Al-Hikma clinic, a private clinic in Insha'at. The staff were overwhelmed, too many wounded that day, they couldn't operate on them. They called another private clinic, Al-Amin, 600 meters away in the same neighborhood. There is a checkpoint between the two clinics. Al-Amin sent a vehicle, marked "medical emergencies," with nurses, to Al-Hikma to bring back the wounded. On the way out the vehicle passed through the checkpoint; on the way back, it is stopped, the soldiers and security forces see the wounded; they make the two men get out and let the woman go on to the clinic. The two men are brought in a tank to the military hospital, in the al-Wa'ar neighborhood, near the Military Academy.

It's Z. who's telling the story, miming some events, waving his hand with the tube from the IV. The wounded had spent 30–45 minutes in the first clinic, but hadn't received any treatment there, except for a tranquilizer. His nephew's arm wasn't completely torn off like Z.'s leg, which had been bandaged by his neighbors with a scarf. At the military hospital, still without having received any treatment, they were handed over to the men in charge of the cells, tied to beds, and tortured right on the beds, for over eight hours. Hit on the body and head with food trays. The nephew, 'Ali, died under the torture. An hour after 'Ali's death, Z. was brought to the operating room where he was finally operated on, an attempt to re-attach the still partly connected leg. Then they brought him to a cell.

In the cell, from lack of care, his leg got infected; six days after his arrest, a military doctor decided they had to cut it off.

In his right leg, three deep scars, the aftermath of an accident twenty years ago. He was already handicapped, his right leg was 17 cm shorter than his left leg. Now, it's the only one left.

Muhammad Z. says: "He's the only person from here we know who left the military hospital alive."

I return to the question of the torture. Z. explains. The torturers didn't ask any questions, just mouthed insults: "Ah, you want freedom, here's your freedom!" They also insulted their wives. During the torture, his face was covered with a blanket, and he couldn't see the people who were beating him.

Z. was accused of taking up arms. He defended himself, saying: "No, that's impossible, I'm handicapped." The people here think that's why his life was spared.

One of the men jumped on his chest with both feet. They attached ropes to his wounded leg and pulled it left and right. "There are a lot of things they did to me, but I don't remember." During those seven or eight hours, he and his nephew were tortured in turns. There were other prisoners in the room, already tortured: "Their case was already settled." Another man of about sixty also died. He had come in wounded in the shoulder, they didn't stop hitting him for an hour until he died. Z. doesn't know who it was, he could just judge his age from his voice.

The torturers signaled their entrance in the room by rattling the door handle, and all the prisoners had to cover their faces with their blankets, under penalty of being executed.

He is sure that the men who tortured him are not doctors. Thinks that they're members of the security forces. He shows us scars on his ankles and others less visible on his wrists, from the chains that bound him.

In all Z. stayed for twenty-five days in the military hospital. He didn't see anyone else die. But one tortured man had his back broken.

When Z. was set free, just a week ago, he was brought to the courthouse and judged: bearing arms, incitation to demonstrate, aid to armed groups, armed insurrection, etc. "The interrogators, they hit you, hit you, hit you and in the end you find yourself with a list of charges in which you don't recognize yourself at all." Freed on bail thanks to the amnesty, but the charges still stand [*this amnesty was promulgated by Bashar al-Assad on January 15, 2012, but it was never really applied*]. Brought back home by his brother in a taxi. He has to present himself before the judge in a month, but thinks he'll send a lawyer to represent him.

On a cellphone, they show us a photo of Z. when he came out of the hospital. Yellow skin, gray beard, features drawn, corpse-like, but obviously quietly happy to be alive. They also show us a photo of a man killed by the shell, the father of one of the men here, and a video of the incident. Horrible, women screaming, a distraught man keeps crying *Allahu Akbar*, you can see several corpses lying around, a man carries a wounded woman to put her in a pickup, the neighbor probably. At the very beginning you see Z., his leg dangling, being bundled by some people into a vehicle.

As we leave, Z. looks at me with shining eyes and blows me a kiss. Then he says: "They killed me, over there. I shouldn't have made it."

———

Around 2:00 PM, in the center of the suburb, a protest demonstration against the report of the Arab League, which the people think is too negative. They want the issue to be transferred from the League to the Security Council.

During the demonstration, an officer is lifted on to people's shoulders and carried with his AK as the people chant "Long live the FSA!" He's a *naqib* who has just deserted. They also chant: "The people want international protection," "The people want a no-fly zone," "The people want the proclamation of jihad."

At the demonstration, Bassam, still just as dignified and charismatic, with his intense eyes. Afterwards we walk a little with Dr. 'Ali and one of his friends. We snack on *ful* from a street peddler, surrounded by kids, many of whom wear blue and orange hats and scarves, the colors of the Al-Karama soccer club, the Homs club whose goalkeeper Abdul Basset al-Sarout has taken position for the revolution.[36] We offer some *ful* to Bassam, but he refuses: he has been fasting for six months, every day except the two Eids, when it's forbidden to fast: "It makes me stronger," he says. Then we go get warm near a brazier. It's still bitterly cold, the sky is gray, drowned in the fog in front of which the nearby buildings and the minarets of a mosque stand out. Migrating birds wheel above the roofs. A few volleys of gunfire, on different sides, then the call to prayer.

It begins snowing large flakes.

Visit in the neighborhood to a man, in his early thirties, who got shot through the face. Healed well, he talks to us, but the right side of his face and especially his eye are terribly swollen. Very tense, is very afraid. He needs two or three operations: one to reset his cheekbone, one for cosmetic surgery, one for the eye; each time he has to go to the ophthalmologist's, going through the checkpoints terrifies him. His wound can't be hidden.

It happened a month and a half ago, on the main avenue, when the checkpoint in the center of Baba 'Amr still existed. Calm day, nothing was happening. He crossed the main avenue with his cousin and the checkpoint began shooting,

---

36 *Note to the Verso edition*: the revolutionary trajectory of Abdul Basset al-Sarout and his friends is the subject of the documentary film *Return to Homs*, directed by Talal Derki and filmed by several people I met in Homs. See the Introduction, as well as the January 29 chapter.

for no reason. They heard bullets whistling around them and began running. Just before reaching the cross street, his head was turned, a bullet entered through the top of his cheek and came out right under his eye. He was handed over to the FSA who transferred him to the Red Crescent, probably around Insha'at. The Red Crescent brought him to the Al-Birr private clinic. At the clinic, there is a police station. They checked he wasn't wanted, filled out a report, but didn't contact the *mukhabarat*. The next day, after the operation, his family quickly came to get him to avoid problems.

He refuses photos, as does his older brother who speaks for him. They're both very afraid.

In the park next door, kids run, play, shout under the wet snow.

The snow quickly stops. As we eat cold falafel in a shop, an explosion, not too far away, followed by gunfire.

We walk around for a bit in the fog, then we find a soldier who offers to show us the detonation site. It's in a narrow alley near the "front," the traffic circle that leads to Brazil Street: two rifle-propelled grenades, close to one of the last FSA posts, one of which didn't explode. We look at the impact and then leave. The soldier, 'Abd al-Qader, declares to us: "You have to leave. Riad al-Asa'ad told us that you can't stay, for security reasons, your own security. The Army might attack the neighborhood just as they attacked Jacquier's group."

As has been said, these tensions with various civilian activists or FSA soldiers were a constant during our visit. Several times, Ra'id had to defend himself against rather brutal attempts to erase some of his files. Each time, Muhannad al-'Umar, from the Military Council, intervened to calm things down, and this is why we once again sought to meet him here.

We call Muhannad: "Go back to Hassan's. I'll come in twenty minutes." We go back. There, Hassan and his friends are waiting for us with a hot roasted chicken and some hummus which I joyfully devour while Ra'id, just in case, makes a copy of all his files.

Arrival of Muhannad. Everyone sits down in a circle and right away things become more formal. Muhannad gently asks Ra'id some questions: Have you seen what you wanted to see? What are your plans? What do you think of the situation? Ra'id explains that the situation is better than on his first visit; thanks to the expulsion of the checkpoint, the neighborhood is safer. We'd like to continue on to al-Khalidiya, then maybe go to Telbisi, to see people he knows, and whom he names. "Who brought you over the Lebanese border?" – "Abu Brahim." It goes on like that. Muhannad asks questions about the problem at the first clinic, with Abu Bari. Ra'id explains: the photos, etc. Muhannad: "You mustn't go anymore to Abu Bari's clinic. That's why we brought you the wounded to the other clinic."

He and Hassan have an exchange about Jeddi, about how poorly he behaved the first day, when he left slamming the door. Muhannad: "It's not appropriate for someone in charge of information, he didn't behave well. He should apologize. The people who behaved badly with you should apologize. If you want to continue, you can continue without any problem, you're welcome. Imad will stay with you and there won't be any problems."

Muhannad talks to us about the criminal police officer, Abu 'Ali Mundhir, who with two *shabbiha* kidnapped four girls. He's the same man the girl at Abu Bari's clinic was talking about. In front of us, he calls the girl, gets the same five names I already have, then a sixth. There are three other girls detained by Mundhir, but they don't have their names. Nine in all.

The sixth girl is the one they had told us about at the Military Council, the girl taken at the hair salon. Muhannad says that yes, when we discussed her they thought she had been taken by the Air Force *mukhabarat*, but now they know it's Mundhir.

Mundhir detains the women for his own purposes, like a *shabbiha*. The FSA has tried to push, via the observers from the Arab League, for them to be transferred to Political Security, but to no avail so far.

Muhammad Z.'s brother, "the sympathetic Salafi" as I call him, is there. His name is Abu Salaam. He explains that his brother's two wives were captured at the end of December by the *shabbiha*, in the orchards. Muhammad is wanted, and the *shabbiha* came for him at his country home; they didn't find him there, and took the two women hostage so he would give himself up. They were held for six days; then, when the observers of the Arab League arrived, they were freed. Muhammad didn't tell us for fear we'd ask to see them.

Muhammad's wives were mistreated, says Muhannad, badly mistreated. No more detail. Too many people in the room to insist.

We return to the question of jihad. Muhannad: "Every day there are deaths. The position of the Arab League is weak, the international position is weak, so the idea of jihad is becoming more unavoidable."

What does that mean? "We want all the fighters in the Arab world to come join us to fight. We want all the authorities who continue working for the state to be punishable by the death penalty. When we proclaim it, all the civilians who haven't yet taken up arms will join us."

For them, there isn't enough international pressure. "If we move to jihad, we move to the stage of militarized revolution."

Imad interrupts: "No, if we do that, we move to general war."

They want a direct intervention by NATO, which was not the case in November. At that time, Ra'id had seen a demonstration in al-Qusur [*a neighborhood in the northwestern part of the city*], where an activist had tried to start the slogan, "The people want NATO intervention!" No one had taken up the slogan, despite all his attempts.

Muhannad: The FSA has kidnapped three men and two women to exchange for sixteen workers from the Mandarin (Pepsi) company taken by the *shabbiha* around November 16. They were arrested at a *mukhabarat* checkpoint, who called the *shabbiha* who took them away. Five days later the

FSA kidnapped the five people, and two days later negotiated an exchange.

Among the two women there was one Alawite and one Ismaili. One was the wife, the other the sister of an officer. The three young men were also Alawite, two *shabbiha* and the owner of a brothel, according to them.

Muhannad thinks that with the hardening of the repression, it's likely they're headed toward a sectarian conflict. "The fact that the Alawite community supports the regime unequivocally can lead to a religious confrontation. But this question lies with the religious leaders, the shaykhs.

"We are conscious that the regime is playing the card of religious confrontation. But if the regime falls, its methods will disappear. There won't be any reprisals. The ones who took part will be judged. The Alawite community will have its share, like all Syrian citizens. In any case, you can't erase them. They're part of Syrian society, like us.

"I know how the people in the Sunni community think. We don't have that sectarian way of thinking."

We have them explain the organization of the neighborhood to us. There are three structures:

- The *Majlis al-'Askari* (Military Council): twenty-four members, including three civilians and twenty-one military.
- The *Majlis ash-Shura* (Civilian Council or Advisory Council), which takes care of questions of justice,

humanitarian aid to civilians, and also supplying the
FSA: fourteen members, seven civilians and seven
military.

- The *tansiqiyat* (local coordination committees), which
organize the demonstrations. The *Maktab Al-I'ilami*
(Information Bureau) is one of these committees.

Muhannad asserts that 'Abd ar-Razzaq Tlass is not the
commander of the *katiba*. He doesn't want to say the name
of the real commander. 'Abd ar-Razzaq Tlass is a member
of the Military Council, but some members have a higher
rank than him, like the *naqib* we saw at the demonstration
(who in fact deserted two months ago).

There is a coordinator, who is a member of the Military
Council – his name is secret – who acts as a link with the
tansikiyyat, and serves as a go-between for the Military
Council, the *tansikiyyat*, and the Syrian National Council.
He's also the one who keeps in contact with Riad al-Asa'ad.

Riad al-Asa'ad gives orders, general directions, and also
weapons and money. They recognize his authority.

The Military Council agrees with the political views and
objectives of the Syrian National Council (SNC). It considers that the SNC represents the revolutionary people,
and accepts its authority. If a transitional government is
constituted, it will bow to its authority.

Arrival of an old gentleman in a suit, very elegant, a retired
officer who begins shouldering sniper rifles and giving
advice. Then a big discussion among the men, Hassan,
Imad, the old man, Abu Jawad, Abu Assad, without the
young men. At the end Abu Jawad and the old man take out

bills, a big wad of Syrian pounds, and give part of it to Hassan, "for the young guys" if I understood right. Hassan tries to refuse, argues, finally the money stays under an ashtray. Then everyone separates and we go to Dr. 'Ali's place to find some internet.

––––––

We end up in a room full of activists, each one with a laptop, working on Facebook or other sites. There is Aloush, who leads the demonstrations, and some friends. A *narghile* is prepared. The connections are very slow but safe, made secure by Tor. But my USB drive has caught a serious virus at 'Abd ar-Razzaq Tlass's place. Impossible to clean it. "I caught it at *al-Jaysh al-Hurr*, the Free Army." – "*Al-Jaysh al-Hurr* is a virus!"

'Ali the living martyr is there. His friends tell us how they thought he was dead. He weighed 100 kg at the time and his buddy Abu Slimane, a skinny little guy, couldn't even manage to haul his body. They took him to the hospital through the checkpoints: when the soldiers saw the state he was in, they let him pass: "In any case, he's already dead."

Rather proudly, the living martyr shows us a video of him just after his injury, half of his left lung coming out of his chest.

According to the youths, there's only been one death since our arrival, Abd al-Kafi M., killed at the military hospital. It's probably the one whose funeral we missed, the one they said had just died. But just before it had been very violent:

five deaths on Sunday the 15th, five deaths on Tuesday the 17th, one dead on Wednesday the 18th, the day before we arrived.

Abu Slimane: "Our parents were submitted through fear. We broke down the wall of fear. Either we will win, or we will die." Makes a V sign with his fingers. Photo session, they all pose making Vs – but only for their cameras, not mine.

Monday, January 23

Baba 'Amr

Rough awakening. Around 10:00, 10:20 AM, I slowly emerge to the sound of distant gunfire. I try to shake Ra'id; Fadi and Ahmad are sleeping in the living room, I go and look for hot water, but there's no more fuel oil. Some guys turn up quickly, a little agitated, they're coming to get machine guns and cartridge belts. The volleys of gunfire continue, most of them rather close it seems, something's happening. The soldiers wake up Fadi and Ahmad, we quickly get dressed and decide to follow them.

Outside, it's cold, wet, and foggy. We cross the little square running toward Hassan's command post, no one. Imad arrives, his car screeching to a halt, explains a little. We start running down the street along the buildings facing the front line, where the shooting positions are set up. The volleys are sustained and very close, it's clearly the FSA shooting now. Ibn Pedro arrives in a car with two buddies and we head into a building, up to the third floor. A young guy is posted at a shell hole with a machine gun, but it is jammed. Ahmad comes up with his and takes his place, then begins firing short volleys. The empty cartridges

bounce off the walls, Ra'id photographs, the racket is deaf-
ening. The others watch calmly, smoking and trading jokes.
Then Ibn Pedro takes Ahmad's place for some practice, a
little morning exercise. The smell of cordite fills the ravaged apartment.

Ibn Pedro explains the situation: a sniper began shooting
at civilians and wounded four. The FSA is returning fire
against the sniper, who is posted in one of the towers near
the stadium.

The first young guy resumes his place and tries to fire.
He lets off a few volleys but his machine gun keeps
jamming.

We go out. The guys in the street are calm, talking. Fadi
arrives. Me: "So, did you find some fuel oil to heat the
water?" Ahmad leaves to go get more ammunition.

We head down the street with Fadi, go through another
building, then pass the garden wall through a hole, to enter
the neighboring building. The staircase window is exposed,
we have to run upstairs. Upstairs is the apartment with the
melted television, with sofas overturned in every direction.
One guy has set up a metal ladder in front of a hole in the
wall, to serve as a support for his gun, and has settled com-
fortably on to a little office chair. Several guys take turns
firing a few shots. I begin to take notes, Ra'id telephones
Imad. There are three FSA wounded, by an RPG, one
pretty seriously. But all the wounded are at Abu Bari's
clinic, we won't have access.

We go back down and out, then climb back up to the
first apartment. Abu Husayn, a stocky, smiling guy with a
beard and bad teeth, wrapped in a traditional pon-
cho-blanket, is shooting very noisily with his G3 Heckler

& Koch. The other guy is still struggling with his jammed machine gun, then lets off a few volleys that echo in the little room.

It's calmed down a little but the guys think the Army is going to start up again. A little earlier there was a rifle grenade explosion, further away, but otherwise no artillery fire. Apparently we're out of range for RPGs. Abu Hussein explains the tanks only fire when they attack. On the other hand if the FSA kills one of theirs they start lobbing mortar shells.

The neighborhood imam launches his call to prayer as if nothing had happened. Some young guys come in and out. 'Alaa has posted himself in front of the firing hole and is smoking.

A lull. Discussion. Abu Mahmud comes in, greets us cheerfully. Another FSA soldier was slightly wounded, glass shards in his forehead. Some soldiers offer to go to Insha'at. "No, stay at your post," orders Abu Mahmud.

It's bitterly cold, the vapor from people's breath rises up in front of their faces, men pace back and forth in the destroyed apartment.

'Ali calls us: there is a *shahid* at the Gilani mosque. We go there at a run so as not to miss the end of the prayer. We arrive all out of breath. In the mosque few people are praying. The corpse is lying in a corner, wrapped in a shroud and placed on a bier. But it seems he died a natural death.

We buy some candy and potato chips at the corner grocery, enough for all the guys, and run back to the buildings at the front. Abu Mahmud has received some information, from a guy just arrived from Insha'at, where the whole thing began, that the Army is going to attack.

In front of his base, Hassan, in a tracksuit, is putting a sniper rifle back together. He confirms the information and advises us to go take shelter in the apartment.

Discussion with Ra'id. Hassan suggests we go join Ibn Pedro who is shooting from inside a building. Ra'id wants to stay with Hassan. In any case there's a pause, there's almost no more gunfire, the men are warming themselves around a brazier.

In front of the building, a KIA with five bullet holes in the windshield, holes in the seats. The driver explains: he was just getting ready to get in when they fired. "*Al-Hamdulillah!*" It happened an hour ago, in Insha'at.

We return to the front of the command post, eating and talking. The chips are vinegar flavored, not very good. Fadi brings some ammunition from the apartment. I go back to rinse my face and get another notebook – this one is almost finished, and it would be a shame to run out just when things are getting interesting. When I return Abu Yazan is there. He's the one who was slightly wounded in the forehead. His friend, in Insha'at, was wounded in the groin by a sniper, and out of anger he fired an RPG through a bay window, which flew into his face.

For now it's still calm. It's about 1:00 PM. Maybe the soldiers have decided to eat before attacking.

Just as I write this, shooting breaks out on all sides. Hassan asks us to step back against the wall. "There could be a grenade." But no one goes inside the command post. The soldiers, apparently, are 100 meters away.

It's still gray out. The sun hangs over the buildings, a pale disk, shining in the fog. The grayish taste of war.

Hassan takes his sniper rifle: "I want to go try it." We pass through the command post apartment, then a garden, a hole in a wall, another devastated apartment. In the living room in the midst of debris, some fine furniture, gilt sofas and armchairs, faux Louis XVI. Some are overturned, one of the armchairs is placed in front of a hole in the wall; Hassan settles into it, takes aim and begins firing shot after shot. The empty cartridges clack against the wall, the smell of cordite fills the room. Hassan has covered his head with Ra'id's *keffiyeh*, so his face won't be visible on the photo, and soon he's stifling. Abu Hussein arrives and takes his place in front of the hole to begin shooting in turn.

They're firing at the enemy position's sandbags, to force the snipers to duck and prevent them from shooting. They don't have sophisticated enough weapons to dislodge them, but occasionally manage to kill one if he shows himself.

Hassan goes upstairs, fires a few more shots through a window in the stairwell on the second-floor landing. We follow him. On the way back down, just as I pass the exposed window, he fires, and I finish my descent at a gallop, to Ra'id's laughter: "Ah, I missed a good photo there."

Outside, arrival of Abu Hassan in a car. Greetings. Abu Hassan to Ra'id: "You're shooting?" Ra'id shows his camera: "I'm shooting."

The shots continue, regular. It goes on like that. We move around, I have time to take notes. The guys, at their positions, shoot regularly. It's that singularly elastic, nervous time of waiting. If the attack starts, it will all go very quickly.

Ahmad, the bearded bear, is Hassan's second-in-command, and commands when he isn't there.

We climb on to a roof where there's another position. 'Alaa is lying with a machine gun and a scope, vaguely protected by three sandbags and a few cinderblocks. I lie down in his place and with the zoom of my Lumix he shows me the position of the enemy sniper, at the end of the street, straight ahead, in a house behind the stadium, 400 meters away.

Through holes in the walls, I also look at and photograph the positions of the snipers in the towers on the right, the one under construction and the one with the blue windows. I can see sandbags, barely 200 meters away, the walls around them riddled with bullets. It's calm, the sun finally comes out and shines on the debris-covered roof, from time to time one of the guys lets off a volley, otherwise we talk. Someone bring us embroidered cushions and we settle against the wall of the stairwell, very much at ease. Someone is making tea, it seems.

All of a sudden all hell breaks loose again, the guys jump to their guns and open heavy fire. The guys opposite fire back and you can hear the bullets whistling by. I draw back behind the stairwell, which isn't very safe either as it's riddled with holes. Ra'id takes pictures. It lasts for about five minutes and then calms down. I go back to sit down: "So, 'Alaa, where's the tea? *Wen chai?*"

'Alaa explains that an unmarked car has arrived at the enemy post, to supply them with ammunition, and they opened fire at it. They think they wounded the men. The enemy post replied to cover their guys. Us: how did you know they were soldiers, if it was a civilian car? They saw a guy in uniform in the car, that's why they fired. They don't fire at civilians, of course, but soldiers confiscate civilian vehicles to supply their positions here. If they come with an armored vehicle, the FSA will take it out with an RPG. Ra'id: "So why don't they dress in civilian clothes as well?" 'Alaa: "They'd risk getting shot at by their own snipers!"

It's very calm again. In the distance, we can hear the traffic on the *autostrad*. The shoes of 'Alaa, still lying down, are losing their soles.

Between the skirmishes, boredom sets in. The guys smoke, chat. It's not so cold now that the sun has come out. We go back to the command post, calmly, to drink tea with Hassan, Imad, and some others. Fadi's mother has made some delicious *empanadillas*[37] with meat and cheese that we eat with piping-hot tea. It's incredibly good, the body relaxes all at once.

Afterwards, return to the house. Hot shower, wonderful. When I come out, Ra'id has left. Sudden feeling of exhaustion. As if I were suddenly melting. It's only then that you feel the tension, when it ebbs.

More firing. Ra'id returns a little later. One of the men was wounded, a bullet in the arm apparently. He describes to

---

37   In Spanish, little stuffed patties.

me an eight-year-old boy who was calmly walking, on the side of the street exposed to the snipers, while there was shooting on all sides.

The soldiers' lives: sleep, eat, clean the weapons, stand watch, and from time to time fight. A lot of patience and boredom for a few intense hours, which sometimes end in a wound, or death.

A young guy I don't know returns to replenish his ammunition. He empties the cartridges from a jute bag and, kneeling on the rug, fills his cartridge clip. Black cap, little moustache, black ammo vest over his windbreaker.

We came back at around 3:00 PM, all this lasted about four hours. Around 4:30 PM, Imad finally brings some *sfihas* and yogurt. Ibn Pedro is there, Ahmad too, some other young guys, everyone eats with gusto. At one point, a big explosion, not far off. Hassan telephones: one of his guys fired an RPG, to dislodge a sniper.

A very curious sense of disconnection during the fighting. The hellish noise of firing gets on your nerves, even though it's friendly fire, without any danger. On the other side, the shots sound like firecrackers, a child's game, for the fun of it. You try to take cover but there are openings everywhere, everything is in a line of fire, you have no real idea of what's safe and what's not. You ask and you have to take others' word for it. All this remains fabulously abstract, even when the guys opposite are shooting at you. It is only, I imagine, when you take a hit that it suddenly and irremediably becomes concrete. But so long as you have nothing there's always a curiously unreal feeling to it all, as if you were moving in a dream, as if everything happening were happening to others, not to you.

Return of Abu Yazan, looking exhausted, with a bandage on his forehead. It's not too serious.

5:00 PM, Imad goes to see the family of the wounded man, and categorically refuses to take us with him. Ibn Pedro starts harassing Ra'id for his photos from his last trip, says someone had problems because of him, which is ridiculous, given the precautions Ra'id takes. He shows them the PDFs and that seems to calm things down. But Ibn Pedro is still annoyed, he doesn't look convinced.

Ra'id: "Sometimes you're lucky not to speak Arabic. The least I can say is that it wasn't very cool. To say that in front of all the others, just like that, it's kind of shitty."

In a corner, the young machine-gunner from this morning is reloading cartridge belts with cartridges taken from a big bag full of ammunition. A few others start doing the same thing.

I go out with 'Alaa to do some shopping. The streets are wet, puddles shine in the headlights. The soldiers at the checkpoints look like ghosts, lighting up their cellphones as flashlights.

I buy some Aleppo soap near the mosque. On the way back, the guys take the piss out of me: "You're with those

from Aleppo, you're with Bashar! You're buying Aleppo
soap, you're a traitor!"[38]

7:30 PM. Impossible to reach or find Abu Salim, the
mukhabarat doctor we'd like to see again.

Around 11:00 PM, a young soldier nicknamed The Cat leads
us on foot to the home of some other activists, for the internet
connection. These guys are violently against the declaration
of jihad: "Our revolution is not a religious revolution, it's a
revolution for freedom. Declaring jihad would completely
change the scope of the message of the Syrian revolution.
Yes, people have chanted the slogan during demonstrations.
But they're simple people, they don't understand."

Our host, Abu 'Adnan, is a Communist lawyer who
defends political prisoners. He suggests taking us to the
courthouse, to see how things work. "With money anything is possible." There's also a cameraman there, Abu
Yazan al-Homsi, who provides a lot of images to Al Jazeera
and other networks.

During the meal, Abu 'Adnan serves us some "whiskey," a
local, somewhat syrupy brew, specifying that we shouldn't
talk about it outside this room, and asks if we believe in

---

38   *Note to the Verso edition*: until Syrian rebels from the surrounding
countryside stormed, in July 2012, over half the city of Aleppo, launching
one of the worst urban battles of the civil war, the city – the economic capital
of Syria where the local middle class had a strong vested interest in a peaceful
status quo – had known hardly any demonstrations, other than a few quickly
repressed attempts by students from the university.

Karl Marx. He believes in Karl Marx the way others believe in Jesus or Muhammad, at least that's what he says. His father, of whom a very formal portrait hangs on the wall, was also a Communist. The pharmacist, 'Abd al-Qadir, corrects his statements: "*Din, din. Fikr, fikr.*" Religion is religion. Thought is thought.

Earlier, Abu Yazan al-Homsi was explaining to Ra'id that he regards himself as an activist, not a journalist. "I could never send an image that might harm the revolution." He can almost never film the FSA. Once, he filmed the destruction of a tank, but the FSA forbade him from sending out the images. The FSA is afraid of showing that there are civilians who joined their ranks. For them that would be giving credit to the regime's claims of "terrorism." Strong paranoia on that level.

Abu Yazan al-Homsi confirms that all the foreign journalists (except for us) work with the Information Bureau. "It's because they can't have access to certain information. The Bureau controls them."

Abu 'Adnan wants to start a conversation with me via Google Translate: "Please tell the world we are not islamists." – "I am a Communist and I hate islamists."

We finally manage to leave around 3:00 AM. Abu 'Adnan, slightly drunk, accompanies us in the street: "When we're free, come back as tourists, you will be my guests!" Return on foot with The Cat, in the bitter cold, through the puddles. The FSA checkpoint is keeping watch and yells at us, "Who goes there?" The Cat answers and doesn't stop.

Tuesday, January 24

Baba 'Amr – al-Khalidiya – al-Bayada

10:00 AM. I wake up as Ahmad and a few guys are already talking loudly around the *sobia*. Fadi is still sleeping. They are drinking maté and we make some tea. Ra'id calls his friend Abu Assad, to organize the crossing over to al-Khalidiya, but it's complicated for him. Finally it's Bilal who will come, an activist from al-Khalidiya who works with the clandestine hospitals.

Despite some unfinished business, like the discussions with the mukhabarat *doctor we were unable to meet again, we had decided the day before to leave Baba 'Amr to begin working in the center neighborhoods, starting with al-Khalidiya which is on the north-west side of the city, where Ra'id had good contacts.*

Around noon, after the prayer, the funeral of a *shahid*. According to the activists from last night he was a civilian who, returning from the center of town, was stopped at a checkpoint, where they saw he lived in Baba 'Amr. At that point gunfire broke out between the checkpoint soldiers and the FSA; the soldiers bound the man and used him as a human shield. He wasn't hit but was executed afterwards.

Wait in front of the mosque in the rain.

According to the information collected, the *shahid* was named Muhammad W. He was buried at 9:00 this morning. But he's not the *shahid* they told us about yesterday, he's a man wounded ten days ago by the shell that fell on the bakery, and who died yesterday from his wounds. [*The bombing, shortly before our arrival, of the bakery in Insha'at, near Brazil Street, caused numerous civilian casualties.*] Ra'id calls back Abu Yazan al-Homsi, the Al Jazeera cameraman: no, this was the *shahid* we were looking for. He was hit four days ago – at the checkpoint, as they told us? Impossible to know – and he died yesterday. Since his family is from al-Wa'er, near the refinery, they took his body this morning to bury it there. Another completely confused story, like all the stories here.

Turns out the dead man from the bakery also exists, and was indeed buried this morning.

Discussion with a group of women: "May God protect you, my sons! May the same thing not happen to you as to your fellow countryman!" A guy on a bike, with shopping bags hanging from the handlebars and wearing earmuffs, joins the conversation. His brother was killed in December by a sniper, as he was taking the bus to go to work.

Since the night of the narghile, *with Dr. 'Ali and the activists, I had developed a cough that would later only worsen and would cling to me for the rest of our stay. Since Ra'id's friend who was to bring us to al-Khalidiya still hadn't arrived, we head off on foot to look for a pharmacy.*

Pharmacy on the main street, where I go to buy some cough syrup. The pharmacist, Ahmad, speaks perfect Russian, he studied in Moscow for ten years, 1990–2000. His brother too, who is a doctor in Damascus. He just reopened the pharmacy a week ago. The whole area had been heavily bombed.

He's almost the first person I can speak directly with since I've been here, and I'm very happy.

Ahmad comes from a village near the Lebanese border, on the road to Tartus. He studied in Saudi Arabia, before Russia, then worked there and in his home village too. He settled in Baba 'Amr five years ago. But he grew up here, his father was a teacher. He is Turkmen, like all the people from his village, a town of 14,000 people.

"I've traveled a lot, Russia, Romania, Greece, Turkey, Saudi Arabia, and I've never seen a government like this." His pharmacy was looted three times by soldiers. The shop window and metal shutters are riddled with bullet and shrapnel holes.

He gets his medicine from the center of town, and also from Damascus, Aleppo, elsewhere; he places the order and they are brought to him, one or two days later. The price of medicine hasn't gone up, he thinks it's still controlled by the Ministry of Health. However, many are very hard to find. They lack everything. Just at that moment a well-dressed man arrives, bringing medicine from the center of town. Ahmed and he discuss the next order. The price of para-medical products (milk for children, bandages, cough drops, etc.), which is not controlled, has increased 100–120 percent. Very dangerous to come from the center.

Ahmad jokes about Russia. Over there they used to say to him, "Ты не пьёшь, ты не куришь, почему живёшь? – Толко штобы бегать за девушками."[39]

Earlier on, he helped Imad's clinic, but it didn't go well. Is reticent to speak about it. Finally lets me know that not everything he gave arrived where it should have. "They're good guys there, but there are internal conflicts. And some profit from them." He doesn't have any more money because of the three lootings, and with this situation as well, he doesn't want to help anymore. "And Abu Bari's clinic?" – "No, never!" Vehement reply.

He talks about his uncle, a pilot. Air Force officers are closely watched. Several colleagues of his uncle wanted to desert, they were caught and killed. The uncle managed to flee, he fought a little with the FSA, now he is hiding in the village.

———

We go to the Military Council to see Muhannad before leaving Baba 'Amr. In the median strip behind the mosque,

———

39 "You don't drink, you don't smoke, why do you live? – Only to chase girls."

between the trees, two graves already dug, waiting, ready. It's for days when there's too much shooting to go to the cemetery.

Photo session in front of the Military Council: portraits of 'Abd ar-Razzaq Tlass, proud and smiling in his uniform, who poses brandishing his Kalashnikov, and of the *naqib* Ayman al-Fadus. Then brief conversation with Muhannad.

Sudden rush of fever during the wait and then the discussion. My whole body vibrating.

———

The passage to al-Khalidiya, around 2:00 PM. An ordinary taxi that comes to pick us up in front of the Military Council, sent by Bilal, Ra'id's friend. We go by the apartment to pick up our bags, quickly because Tlass is leaving to launch an attack against some Army checkpoints and things might go sour, and we leave. As soon as we reach Insha'at the topology of the city changes, the buildings are cleaner, there are sidewalks, trees, lawns, many more people, many more cars. We veer into an avenue: in front of us, a building surmounted by an immense portrait of Assad senior, the Ba'ath headquarters apparently. We are obviously no longer in friendly territory, but we don't see any soldiers, any checkpoints.

Feeling that the fever is reflecting my state of mind, feverish and fragile.

The taxi heads up the avenue, the traffic is dense, the buildings are full of shops, there are people everywhere. All the

pro-opposition neighborhoods are full of piles of trash
bags and garbage: the municipality has stopped picking up
the trash in the opposition neighborhoods as "punishment."
But otherwise we're crossing an animated, "modern"
Syrian city, a thousand miles from Baba 'Amr, a working-class neighborhood from the depths of the city, the
kind of place where normally you never set foot. We go by
Dublin Street, the Corniche, a big avenue in the center of
town, then we weave through little streets to skirt round
some checkpoints, through pro-opposition but non-se-
cured neighborhoods. In twenty minutes, more or less,
we're in al-Khalidiya. There, first surprise: an FSA checkpoint at the entrance to the neighborhood, with sandbags
and armed guys. Ra'id is surprised, that didn't exist in
November; it means the FSA has got seriously stronger, if
they dare show themselves openly here, so close to the
center. This post was set up two days ago; a little further
on, there's another one, in place for a month. It protects the
access to the central square, where the demonstrations take
place. We get there pretty quickly. I'm shaking with fever,
and devour a kind of small cheese pizza with spicy sauce,
cooked in front of me by a street vendor, as we wait for
Bilal who arrives with his spirited friend Zayn. Zayn is
veiled, but dressed in jeans and mountain boots, something
you'd never see in Baba 'Amr. One of Bilal's arms is in a
cast, he got shot while going to save a wounded man, four
days ago.

First big visible difference with Baba 'Amr: the presence of
women. In Baba 'Amr, other than during demonstrations,
they're almost invisible, whereas here they're everywhere,

mingling with the men. It's from details like this that you realize how conservative a neighborhood Baba 'Amr is.

———

Around 3:00 PM, visit to a clandestine health center with Bilal. They serve us some tea, and Zayn shows me a long video clip on her smartphone, filmed by her in this very place, of a taxi driver hit by a bullet in the face dying on the floor in front of the sofa where I'm sitting, as the doctors try desperately to keep him alive by intubating him and performing heart massages. The man is lying in a pool of blood, his brain half on the ground. He dies.

She shows me another film of the corpse of a young guy with a well-groomed beard, killed the same day as the taxi driver. He was an FSA soldier, Abu Saadu, who had gone to speak with the *mukhabarat* soldiers at a post to convince them to join the FSA. One *mukhabarat* put down his gun and told him: "OK, I'll join you." Abu Saadu approached and the *mukhabarat* took out a hidden pistol and killed him with a bullet to the eye. Video of another dead young man, hit in the throat by a sniper, of a veiled activist, her face hidden by sunglasses, pumping up a crowd with a mic in front of the mother and the son of a martyr.

One of the nurses used to work with the Red Crescent. At a checkpoint, they were told: "We shoot at them, and you save them." She explains the Red Crescent can't come to all the neighborhoods, they get shot at regularly. So they agree by phone on a rendezvous with the local doctors, who bring them the wounded person at a safe place.

Bilal's injury. The Army had wounded a man with a bullet to the neck. They thought he was dead. They transported him to another place, put him on the ground, then called Bilal or one of his contacts so they'd come get him, in order to trap him. Bilal came with a friend, the Army was waiting for them and opened fire. –

To be continued, as a wounded man arrives in a car, he's carried into the center and laid face down. He moans, cries: "Allah, Allah!" He has a bullet in the lower back. Young, fat, bearded, about thirty, his arms hang over the sides of the table. He can't feel his legs. Very little blood. Gasps, groans. His belly hurts. Bilal asks him: "Are you wanted?" – "No." Bilal calls the hospital, he has to be evacuated ASAP.

Probably paralyzed. Injection, IV drip. "My belly, my belly," the man keeps moaning. Isn't bleeding much, the bullet is lodged inside. Hit the spinal column. The Red Crescent arrives quickly, in seven to eight minutes, and evacuates him. Takes his identity card.

Welcome to al-Khalidiya.

The nurse who talks to us, after, Abu 'Abdu, used to work in the Al-Birr private clinic, in the Al-Wa'ar neighborhood. Also at the Bab as-Sba'a hospital. Has seen this kind of case often, 150 to 200 at least. Thinks the snipers aim for the spinal column. They're little bullets, sniper bullets, not stray Kalashnikov bullets. Has also seen many people wounded by what he calls explosive bullets, maybe dum-dums.

Bilal shows me his phone again. A man with his whole stomach open, lungs and guts all outside that the doctors shove back in. All these phones are museums of horrors.

Bilal's story, continued. When the Army opened fire, Bilal ran to escape the ambush. He knocked on doors and begged people to open up, no one opened, finally he knocked down a door to get into an apartment. That's when he took the bullet in the arm. The Army began machine-gunning the apartment. A little six-year-old girl got hit in the leg. She was crying, "Uncle, uncle, I've never been to the demonstrations." He had already called the FSA, who sent, he said, 200 men in reinforcement. Some entered the apartment from the rear and gave him a weapon. They counter-attacked the Army to recover the wounded man. This is the moment we see in the film Bilal shows us, where he's firing. They succeeded, and the wounded man, miraculously, survived.

This health center used to be a hair salon. Open for two months already. There is another one in al-Khalidiya. The center Ra'id used to know was discovered by the *mukhabarat*, who arrested the doctor, confiscated the supplies, and put seals on the door. There are no doctors in the clandestine hospitals, the only doctor was arrested. Six colleagues of Abu 'Abdu were also arrested, and he left his hospital from fear of being arrested as well.

———

Bilal takes us just beyond the limit of the neighborhood, to al-Bayada where we're going to stay. He has a nice car, a big 4×4 with leather seats, automatic, he's obviously a man with means. We quickly cross an avenue, where an Army check-point sits 100 meters away, then we enter a dense neighborhood, with FSA men here and there. The apartment was lent by a friend who went on a trip, and left the keys to house wounded men; there's one in the bedroom sleeping, wounded two weeks ago by bullets to the chest and stomach.

Here, it's the Caucasian[40] quarter. 'Arif, a young little guy in *keffiyeh* sitting with us, is of Adyghe ancestry. As for Bilal, he is Bedouin.

I still have fever and ask them to go buy me some ibuprofen. I try to hand them a bill. Bilal: "If you offer money, it's because you're greedy. Because when I come to visit you, you won't offer hospitality."

Explanations from Bilal. The officers at the checkpoints are changed every two weeks. When they're Army officers, it's OK, it's calm. When they're from the *mukhabarat*, there's shooting all the time. Now, on Cairo Avenue, the big street we just crossed, it's a *mukhabarat*. Yesterday they didn't stop shooting, for three hours the sniper didn't let anyone cross.

———

7:00 PM. Still fever. It's time for the demonstration. We go to the central square in al-Khalidiya. The people aren't

---

40 *Note to the Verso edition*: a substantial number of Syrians are the descendants of various Circassian tribes, chased out of the Caucasus Mountains by the Russians in the mid nineteenth century and resettled throughout the Ottoman Empire.

here yet, just a few dozen youths listening to revolutionary music, too loud but very catchy, on the loudspeakers. The square, called the Garden of the Hills, has been renamed the Square of Free Men. In one corner has been erected a wooden copy, painted black and white, of the old central clock of Homs, situated on a square where a few months ago a sit-in attempt was repressed in a bloodbath by the forces of Maher, Bashar's brother. Meaning of this copy: the center of town, now, is *here*. The clock is covered with photos of martyrs, most of them in color, A4 format.

Big rectangular square, with grass and trees, surrounded by heaps of trash bags piled in the street. On one side, a large banner: "No to the imaginary opposition, a creation of al-Assad's gangs. The SNC unites us, factions disperse us." Clear allegiance of the demonstrators to the Syrian National Council. Aside from the clock corner, illuminated by the demonstration spotlights, everything is plunged in darkness. Just a few shops, a barbershop with a beautiful red armchair, stand out in the darkness, passersby appear as ghostlike shadows in the car headlights.

The clock is surrounded by street vendors, that's where we had met Bilal when the taxi dropped us off. Ra'id finds a little blond boy he had photographed in November, with very red fingers and a joyous smile. Many things have changed since then; the information activists, now, film without hiding their faces. The boy is eleven and is named Mahmud. He exclaims: "How did you get back to your country without getting caught at the checkpoints? You're a strong man, a hero."

The crowd gathers and the demonstration takes shape. The leader lists the cities that have risen up: "Idlib, we are with you until death! Telbisi, we are with you until death! Rastan, we are with you until death!" and so on.

A kid begins singing in an artificial, rasping voice, and the dances in rows begin.

> The leader: "We are not rebelling against the Alawites or the Christians. The people are one!"
>
> Everyone: "The people, the people, the people are one!"
>
> Leader: "We count only on God, not on the Arab League, not on the observers, not on NATO!"
>
> Everyone: "We count only on Allah!" (×3)

The extraordinary thing about these demonstrations is the power they let loose. It's a collective, popular jubilation, a jubilation of resistance. And they don't just serve as an outlet, as a moment of collective release for all the tension accumulated day after day for eleven months; they also give energy back to the participants, they fill them every day with vigor and courage to continue to bear the murders, the injuries, the grief. The group generates energy, then each individual reabsorbs it. This is also the purpose of the chants, the music, and the dances, they are not just challenges and slogans, they are also – precisely like the Sufi *dhikr* whose form they take – generators and captors of force. This is how the people hold and continue to hold, thanks to joy, to song and to dance.

———

Internet café, a little further on at the end of a street. According to one guy, thirty-nine dead today in Homs, including twenty-three in Bab Tadmur. The Army bombarded.

This internet café is the meeting place for all the activists in al-Khalidiya, who come to post on YouTube and social networks their work of the day, films of demonstrations or atrocities. Ra'id had spent quite some time here in November, and had stayed for a while in an apartment just above it, from whose balcony he had managed one day to photograph armored vehicles of the security forces carrying out a raid. I check my e-mails, reply to some, then write down the description of the passage from Baba 'Amr to al-Khalidiya.

11:00 PM. A friend of Bilal comes for us at the internet café in a van. When we leave, he turns on the dome light, to pass an FSA checkpoint, then turns everything off, including the headlights, and we cross Cairo Avenue in the dark, as fast as possible. In the apartment, there's still no electricity.

In fact, there's no electricity at all in this neighborhood. A tank destroyed the transformer.

Bilal recounts: three days ago the *shabbiha* chloroformed and kidnapped, in Insha'at, a lawyer who was defending political prisoners, and beat her very violently.

The officer in charge of the FSA in al-Khalidiya is the *mulazim awwal* Umar Shamsi. Ra'id knows Shamsi, he photographed him around Telbisi in November. He was part of the Khalid ibn al-Walid *katiba*. He was invited to come to al-Khalidiya, to train the soldiers. There are now regular exchanges of officers between the *katibas*.

This is an important point. The FSA, in the beginning, was organized on a highly territorial basis: when officers defected, they would return to their home areas and take command of the soldiers of the village or the neighborhood, like Hassan in Baba 'Amr, who commands the troops in the neighborhood where he lives. As someone would explain to me a few days later, the invitation made to Umar Shamsi to come from Telbisi to Khalidiya is the sign of a step forward in the professionalization of the FSA.

Bilal: the victim from this afternoon remained paralyzed. He was crossing between Qusur and Khaldiye, and he was hit. The only victim at that place, the sniper just shot for no reason.

Since Bilal's incident, when they go to pick up the injured outside of al-Khalidiya, they take an FSA car with five men inside as an escort.

Yesterday, there were five dead in Homs.

Wednesday, January 25

Bayada – Safsafi – Bab as-Sba'a – Safsafi

Late awakening, 11:00 AM. Still feverish. We get ready quickly. Ra'id asks Bilal about the twenty-three dead from yesterday. "Already buried." That seems absurd to us.

Excursion in a taxi with Abu 'Adnan, an activist friend of Ra'id. We're going to see a funeral in Safsafi, at the edge of the Alawite neighborhoods. Drive through the center and the old town. The great Khalid ibn al-Walid mosque, unreal in the mist, in the middle of a park. The building of State Security. Then we enter the souk, dense, thick, animated, a labyrinth of shops. There are FSA men here, but hidden. Army sniper opposite, on a building. Normally he doesn't shoot. But if there's a confrontation, he shoots so that the people will run away. There was a battle here three days ago. The security forces are just to the right, 100 meters away. We turn left and dive into the souk. Traffic-jammed labyrinth, mountains of trash fill the streets. The people try to evacuate part of it themselves, but can't keep up. After the shops, a little further on, an

FSA post. Framed calligraphy hanging on the sandbags: "Freedom is a tree that is watered with blood." We arrive at a house in the back of an alleyway, an old-fashioned house with a beautiful paved inner courtyard, where we find old friends of Ra'id's. Of course we've arrived too late for the funeral. We talk in the courtyard. One guy pulls out a bag full of remains of various shells fallen in the neighborhood. Above the courtyard, the sky is gray, sticky. Everything is damp.

Discussion about the dead and the lightning-fast funerals. Abu Bilal [*an activist from Safsafi, not to be confused with Bilal*] explains that the funerals are no longer the way they used to be, they no longer turn into demonstrations: the cemetery is completely exposed, and the snipers on the Homs citadel shoot if there's a crowd. So they bury in small groups, quickly.

Thus everything is hard to verify. This is what explains the difference between the numbers provided by the Syrian Observatory for Human Rights (SOHR) and those we hear about here, since the SOHR only publishes confirmed numbers. For yesterday the SOHR says one dead in Homs. But our friends insist that in Bab Tadmur there were dozens. One building, targeted by the shelling, collapsed, and they're still pulling corpses out of the rubble; another, known to shelter activists, was targeted by a booby-trapped package. We will go see them.

One activist: "You're not from the *Figaro*, at least? *Le Figaro* is really rotten." It's OK, we're from *Le Monde*.

This remark is a direct reference to the article written by Georges Malbrunot in Le Figaro *on January 20, 2012, blaming the FSA for Gilles Jacquier's death, on the basis of an anonymous source in Paris citing an anonymous source in Homs. The editorial board of* Le Monde *asked Georges Malbrunot to share the name of his source, so that Ra'id and I could go talk directly with him on site; alleging his source's safety, Georges Malbrunot refused to accept this request. A detailed article published in* Le Monde *on January 23, 2012 places the information published by* Le Figaro *in the context of all the information then available, which tends, taken as a whole, strongly to implicate the Syrian regime in the death of the French journalist and the eight Syrians killed at the same time.*

The house is in a little street defended by two FSA checkpoints, one at each end. Ra'id goes to photograph one, and this provokes another endless argument with the soldiers, who don't agree.

Another activist calls to complain about how Ra'id was treated by the soldier. "We bring you a friendly journalist and you behave badly."

Return to the checkpoint. Everything is settled. *Shabbiha* checkpoint just to the left, a little further on.

————

We leave in a taxi to go further on, to Bab as-Sba'a. We're with Abu Bilal and also Umar Talawi, an activist known for his video appearances; he has already been on TV, on Al Jazeera and France 24.

According to them, we are the first foreign journalists to come here. At one street corner, a completely destroyed store, riddled with thousands of bullets. On the wall next to it, graffiti in green, "Beware – sniper." *Shabbiha* checkpoint up the side street, 100 meters away, they fire all the time; a vague pile of sand blocks the entrance to the street, to shield people and passing cars a little.

On the main street, further ahead, FSA soldiers.

Visit to the cemetery, magnificent with its old gravestones in the grass, against a foggy background. The citadel and its snipers are just behind, 200 meters away, invisible in the fog. But apparently they can see us, we have to cling to the walls and be very careful about holes. Machine-gunned houses, with traces of RPG impacts. On one side of the cemetery, a wide hole in the wall, recently made to give access to a section sheltered from fire, for funerals.

Return toward the main street. At an FSA checkpoint, a soldier calling himself Abu Ahmad (from Nasihin, a neighborhood of Homs) shows us his Army card: "They brought us into the streets to fight armed gangs. I didn't see any armed gang. They said to us: ammunition isn't worth anything, shoot, shoot as much as you can." That's why he deserted. "They gave us rifle grenades and said to us: Shoot! They took me to Rastan on June 1st. There was no military resistance, no one was shooting, there was nothing but peaceful demonstrators. The Army began shooting with *Shilkas*[41] and BMPs, with rifle grenades. Me, I didn't

---

41   *Shilka* is the Russian name for the ZSU-23-4 or *Zenitnaya Samokhodnaya Ustanovka*, "Anti-Aircraft Self-Propelled Mount," a radar-guided anti-aircraft weapon system of Soviet manufacture, lightly armored and fitted out with four 23 mm cannons. The Syrian Army has apparently used them to fire against ground targets in urban combat situations.

shoot. I shot myself in the leg." He shows us the scar. "We stayed for eight days in Rastan. Then we went to al-Wa'ar. I shot myself on September 26th, when they wanted to send us to Rastan for the second time." Claims he never shot at the crowd, that he hid. That doesn't seem very credible, given he was in operations for four months.

This is a mixed neighborhood, Christian as well. "The Christians are our brothers." one hundred meters further on, Nezha, an Alawite neighborhood. That's where the *shabbiha* checkpoints are.

Bilal Z. Special Forces soldier. Young, almost beardless, just a vague moustache. Sent to Homs for the repression: "I didn't shoot at the people, I shot in the air." He saw one soldier who refused to shoot at the people, saying: "They're just civilians," and they shot him in the leg. But they didn't kill him.

A woman in a *niqab*: "In this street, in every house there is a martyr. Soon it will be a year this has gone on. When is it going to stop? We can't walk in the street safely anymore." Shrill, plaintive voice. Well-dressed, good-quality coat, but you can only see her eyes: "We're people who work, but we can't even feed ourselves. We've come to depending on donations. Let our voices be heard!"

In a street in front of a private hospital, people wait to buy fuel oil, with dozens of jerrycans lined up on the ground.

Visit to the private hospital of Bab as-Sba'a. On the fourth floor, bullet holes in the doors and windows, fired from the citadel. There are seven nurses left, one emergency care doctor, two gynecologists, and one anesthesiologist.

They no longer accept patients, or in any case they can't keep them, from fear they'll be wounded by the gunfire. They accept only emergency cases, and keep people just one day maximum. The beds are empty, it's the nurses, veiled but faces uncovered, who explain. One of the young activists keeps filming us as we talk, it's a little annoying but he says it's just for him.

The hospital can't put up sandbags against the gunfire, since Security regularly makes raids. If they see sandbags, they'll accuse the staff of taking care of activists or soldiers. State Security has come by eight times, the last time was fifteen days ago. Three months ago, they arrested a member of the staff who does blood tests, and accused him of doing analyses on FSA soldiers. He denied it, but they kept him for a month, and tortured him with electricity, pouring water on his body. When he got out he left the country, fled to Jordan.

None of the doctors or nurse practitioners can work at the hospital anymore. They had to sign a promise not to give medical attention to anyone.

We hear a loud impact. It's the citadel that's just shot at the hospital. Everyone laughs.

Since the FSA took up positions in the neighborhood twenty days ago, they can bring sick and wounded people to the hospital. It's the FSA that brings blood and doctors when necessary. But they're afraid of a real military operation, with armored vehicles; the FSA won't be able to withstand that.

Many supply problems. Problems also in getting

specialized doctors to come, because of the checkpoints. Last Saturday, they received a man with his belly torn open. A surgeon managed to operate, to remove the bullets, but they needed a second specialist to finish the operation. He was supposed to come from another neighborhood, but Bab as-Sba'a was surrounded by security forces, impossible to get him in. They tried to transfer the patient in an ambulance to another clinic, also impossible. In the end he died.

As we leave, a throng around the truck distributing fuel oil. Packed together in the hard rain around the small truck, men yell at each other vehemently. But many are laughing too, it's hard to tell if it's serious. The line seems rather orderly. 'Umar, filmed by another activist, gives a brief speech in front of the line, in the rain.

At this stage, we hadn't yet eaten anything all day, and are very hungry. On the main street, near the hospital, a little store was selling shish tauk, *chicken skewers, ready made. But after a discussion with 'Umar, the seller told us they were all pre-ordered, and 'Umar insisted we come to his fiancée's house to eat: "Everything is ready," he promised us.*

Wait at the home of 'Umar's fiancée [*who remained locked up in the kitchen, and whom we would never see*]. 'Umar is wanted, there's two million on his head. Me: "Two million dollars or Syrian pounds?" – "Pounds." – "Oh, that's nothing then." Laughter. 'Umar's five brothers and his father are also wanted. State Security came to his place nine times, they broke and looted everything, the apartment is empty. Before, he had a store, he sold air conditioners.

They broke everything in his store too. He is twenty-four or twenty-five.

A young boy joins us, Muhammad, the brother of 'Umar's fiancée. He is fourteen. His brother Iyad, twenty-four, was killed last week. Three bullets. He shows us the places: side, shoulder, and leg. He was walking with his family near the cemetery, the Army was advancing to enter the neighborhood, and they began shooting. Muhammad was there with his parents and sister. A friend of Iyad's was also wounded. There was no FSA there, no resistance, the soldiers shot for no reason. Iyad didn't die right away, the family took him and fled at a run; they managed to carry him to the hospital, further down, but they couldn't get any medical care for him as the Army entered the building. They managed to evacuate him through a back door and take him to a neighboring apartment; by the time a doctor arrived, it was too late. They buried him in a very small group, with just four people. That's when, from fear of snipers, they dug the hole in the wall of the cemetery, through which we had looked a little earlier on.

The boy tells all this very calmly, without any apparent emotion, in a reedy child's voice. Even here in the warm room he keeps his gloves and hat on. His complexion is quite yellow, but I don't know why.

There is also his little brother Amir, four years old. Muhammad to his brother: "What do the people want?" – Amir, in a tiny voice: "The people want the fall of the regime!"

Muhammad hasn't gone to school for four months. Soldiers and *shabbiha* came and took four children away.

The teacher protested but they threatened him: "Mind your own business and shut up!" There were a lot of them. Muhammad doesn't know the names of the children arrested and doesn't know what happened to them. At that time, the children from the schools were going out to demonstrate; those four must have been denounced for having taken part.

Ra'id asks him: "How did you know they were *shabbiha*?" – "They had big beards and shaved heads." According to Ra'id, that's the typical look for the *shabbiha*, an Alawite gangster look.

Finally, we won't be able to go back to al-Khalidiya today. We'll sleep at the house in Safsafi, in the old city, near the FSA posts. Problem of our bags. We should have kept them with us, but no one told us. The driver who could bring them isn't free.

It is 4:00 PM and we still haven't eaten anything. That doesn't help my state. At 3:00 PM 'Umar had said: "*Wallah*, it's ready, it's ready," and I remind him. Abu Bilal: "He's an information professional. He lies a lot." More laughter.

Discussion about jihad. They don't want a declaration of jihad. It would only make the crisis worse. It would internationalize it, bring in Saudi Arabia, Iran, etc. Lots of foreign groups would like to come fight here, the revolution would get out of the hands of the Syrian people.

Us: "That's what we tried to explain to 'Abd ar-Razzaq Tlass. But he wouldn't listen, he didn't want to understand this."

Ra'id: "You have a more advanced political awareness than the military."

These guys want a NATO intervention.

Finally, at 4:30 PM, we eat. Muhammad's father has arrived in the meantime and eats with us, a dignified gentleman, with white hair and a white moustache, who hides his sadness. The meal, which took a long time in spite of 'Umar's promises, is magnificent: chicken with sauce, bulgur with meat, white beans in sauce that's poured over the bulgur, white radishes, scallions, olives.

———

Afterwards, we go back out, to return to the house of the activists in Safsafi, in old Homs. We find an FSA soldier who has a car and we go up the main street. At the end, there is a mosque they want to show us, riddled with bullets. It's already dark out and they turn on the car's headlights so we can see. The sniper is a little further up to the right; the soldier stands at the corner and shouts as loudly as he can, "Go ahead, shoot, you bloody pimp!" In spite of repeated cries and insults, the sniper doesn't shoot. Then we leave. We take a perpendicular street, sloping down, long and straight, the soldier turns off his headlights and accelerates, the street is narrow and we go at top speed, the guy next to me murmurs: "*Bismillahi ar-Rahman ar-Rahim*," then we cross a wide avenue fast as an arrow, almost invisible in the grayness of the night, to plunge into a little street opposite where the soldier slams on the brakes as he switches the headlights back on. We stop two meters away from the wall of a mosque; on a pole, just in front of us, several tires are hanging: "For the cars that don't brake in time." Everyone bursts out laughing.

The avenue separating Bab as-Sba'a from Safsafi is under fire from a checkpoint, it's the only way you can pass from one neighborhood to another, here. The people call that a *shari' al-mout*, a "street of death."

Then we go to the activists' house, their HQ in Safsafi. In the room in back, well heated, three laptops with internet. Two young guys pray while I write and Ra'id consults his e-mail.

6:00 PM. Arrival of the FSA commanders of the neighborhood. They want to know who we are and what we're doing here. Ra'id explains.

They don't want us to show photos of the checkpoints here, for the neighborhood isn't completely liberated and they don't want to give a false impression. Not liberated means there are still security forces in the neighborhood, checkpoints, unlike Baba 'Amr where the checkpoints are all outside. "Do you plan on attacking the checkpoints, dislodging them?" – "Yes, *insha'Allah*." There are skirmishes every day already. At the beginning, the Army and the *shabbiha* used to enter the neighborhood and attack the demonstrations. When the FSA began to resist, they sent in armored vehicles. That's why they built the checkpoints, to delay the armor. They also have some RPGs. Small exchange about tactics. For them Molotovs are useless against armored vehicles.

Seventeen FSA groups in the neighborhood, the number of men varies. Abu Ammar, a thin young civilian, with a

sparse beard and hollow features, commands a group of
thirty men.

Another officer complains about the guys in Bab as-Sba'a
wasting ammunition. Every night, an Army soldier
approaches the edge of the neighborhood and fires an RPG,
then runs away. The FSA soldiers turn up and empty their
clips into the night. "It's stupid, it doesn't serve any
purpose."

The most dangerous thing for them is the snipers. At
night, as soon as there's any movement, the snipers shoot.
People can't go anywhere. That's why they're leaving the
neighborhood.

The Army checkpoints in the neighborhood are set up in
houses which they emptied of their inhabitants. Sandbags
in front and armored vehicles around. Very hard to get
close. At night, the snipers take their places. The people
who live nearby had to leave their homes, too dangerous.
But since the FSA took up their positions, a month and a
half ago, some people were able to go back home. The FSA
has a dozen checkpoints in the whole area of the old town,
Homs *al-qadimeh*: Bab as-Sba'a, Safsafi, Bab Drib, Bab
Houd, Bab Tadmur, Bab el-Mazdud. In the same zone,
there are about fifteen checkpoints of the security forces.

Labyrinth of little streets, dilapidated houses and little
old-fashioned buildings. One of the officers: "The old town
also has the peculiarity of having a lot of Christians. On
Hamidiya Street, a heavily Christian commercial street, the
FSA had a good understanding with the people. Twenty
days ago, the Army attacked, occupied the street and set up
checkpoints. Since then, the Christians have been com-
plaining: they can no longer circulate freely, the Army

behaves badly with the women, and at night, you can't move around anymore; many want to leave the neighborhood, but the FSA is trying to convince them to stay, saying they'll be setting up positions."

Discussion with an officer who introduces himself as Abu Layl, "the father of night": "There aren't any Christians in the FSA. They remain neutral. They take part in the demonstrations, but don't join the armed struggle. They're a minority and are afraid of government reprisals. They live in protected neighborhoods."

———

Evening demonstration in Safsafi, at 7:00 PM. Small, about a hundred people maybe on a little square, but the same intense energy as everywhere else. Youths and children mostly. Young guys surround me, want to speak their five words of English with me. Everyone shows me his scars, bullet or truncheon injuries. One explains to me that his brother was killed by a sniper from the citadel, as he was driving his car, for nothing. As soon as you arrive somewhere, everyone wants to tell their story right away.

The leader here, a young guy standing on a ladder, *misbaha* in hand, is a more gifted singer than average. He comes to see me when another one takes his place. He speaks rudimentary but understandable English: "Next week I go Saudi Arabia. Please do not show face. Wednesday I go. Face big problem."

Another guy: "Assad Army see us, shoot. This why we here. We can't go wide road. They shoot."

Same slogan as every day: "No-fly zone, international protection."

———

On one of the activist's computers, photos of all the papers, visas, and authorizations of a certain Pierre Enrico Piccinin, a Belgian journalist apparently (born in Gembloux!) who entered Syria officially, then slipped away from his group one afternoon to come to Homs. Little video shot in Bayada, where he explains in French what he's doing there.

9:30 PM. Visit to the underground printing press of Abu Ayham, a young man who speaks a little French. It's a far cry from the underground printing presses of the Resistance, the hand-operated presses of Marc Barbezat or Minuit: a computer connected to a big Encad 736, capable of printing in color on plastic sheets 90 cm wide. This is where they make the posters and banners for the demonstrations, with slogans or caricatures like that of Bashar, presently on the screen, who says with a head like an unscrewed lightbulb: "I think, therefore I'm a jackass."

The poster they're printing now is for the FSA checkpoints. It says, below the logo: "To the officers and soldiers of the Army: We call on you to join the free officers to protect the people."

Outside, regular fire coming from the citadel. The FSA doesn't reply. They're just nuisance shots. But, one of the guys points out, people regularly get killed like that, even though they have nothing whatsoever to do with the revolution.

This same man shows us a wad of 500 Syrian pound

notes. They're coarse counterfeits, full of mistakes. He got them at the bank and doesn't understand how.

We go out and head to the checkpoint a little further on. Two soldiers are warming themselves at a brazier. One of them has a night-vision scope, which I try out. It's my first time and the result is astonishing: you see just as in broad daylight, but in green. Everything is sharp, precise, the fog doesn't interfere at all. All of a sudden you realize how the guys on the other side can see everything – night protects you from nothing.

I ask if with that we could go look at the famous citadel, which I still haven't seen. They take us into a little street to the left of the checkpoint. Just as we enter it, a huge explosion, very close. Cries, alarms. "The wise Peripatetic does not exempt himself from perturbations, but he moderates them" (Montaigne). No wounded. We continue on while Ra'id goes back to photograph. We knock on the door of a building and Abu Layl takes me up to the roof, five floors up. You have to be careful when you look, the citadel is on one side, an Army post on the other. Even without the scope the beauty of the spectacle is unreal, a chaotic panorama of roofs lit up here and there by rare lights, orange in the mist, with minarets rising above them, all around us. Abu Layl first tries to show me the checkpoint but despite the scope I don't see it. The citadel is on the other side, a dark, immense mass bristling with antennas and also with trees, much closer than I thought, 300 meters maybe. I don't look for long. We go back downstairs, greeting the inhabitants who have come out on to their landings. At one landing, a young man standing on a chair, flashlight between his teeth, is trying to repair the building's circuit breaker. In the street, everything is quiet. I go back to the house as Ra'id continues to photograph.

The house, I realize, is not just the HQ of the activists, but also of the neighborhood FSA. One of the rooms, padlocked, but with a glass door, contains their arsenal: two RPGs, a dozen Kalashnikovs, a few M-16s, discernible through a thin curtain.

A little later one of the activists brings the remains of the RPG that just exploded. The head still smells of cordite. Ra'id, when he comes back, tells me it exploded against a wall of the old town, without any damage aside from a Suzuki truck, all of whose windows were shattered. Just next to the impact there is an archway closed by sandbags: maybe the soldiers thought it was an FSA position.

Afterwards, work on the computers. I install Google Earth and they show me where we were today. "The avenue of death" between the Safsafi and Bab as-Sba'a neighborhoods actually runs straight to the citadel.

Not a single woman in this house. This afternoon, when we ate at 'Umar's in-laws', the women remained hidden in the kitchen. I never saw his fiancée. The only women we spoke with today are the two nurses at the hospital and the furious housewife, in a *niqab*, in the street. It's really quite close to Afghan-style *purdah*.[42]

---

42 Persian word for "curtain," which designates the strict separation of the sexes in certain Muslim cultures.

A little after midnight, dinner in the big room, with about twenty FSA men. A veritable feast, there's everything: omelet, cold bean salad, cheese, *labneh*, *mutabbal*, little warm *sfihas*, and halva for dessert. One of the men calls himself Abu Mout, the Father of Death. His three brothers are dead, and his mother took a vow to cook every day for the FSA soldiers, until the end of the revolution. The men bring her the produce and she prepares all of it.

We sleep in the room in back, the HQ of the activists, grouped around the stove, with Abu Bilal.

Thursday, January 26

Safsafi – Bab Drib – Karam
al-Zaytun – Bab Tadmur – Safsafi

Difficult night. Insomnia, then extravagant dreams, the impression of not having slept at all. 'Umar Talawi worked on his computer until almost 4:00 AM, illuminated only by the light from the screen. At dawn I wake again. Cold light, voices. Shooting, not Kalashnikov volleys, but single shots, sniper fire. I wonder if they hit home. Around 9:30 AM I'm awakened again by Abu Bilal's phone and I shake him. Someone he knows has been killed, but he doesn't know who. By one of the shots I heard? Another phone call: it's one of his neighbors, a twelve-year-old child, from Bab Drib. They shoot at kids too. For no reason, no reason whatsoever. Unless it's to punish these stubborn, cursed people, guilty of refusing to bow their heads and obey in silence their lord and master. To punish them slowly.

We fold the blankets and leave to see the boy's body.

But before that, as someone goes to look for a car, a stroll through the neighborhood. Everything is misty, humid. I am shown the impact of yesterday's RPG, on an ancient stone street gate. Then we cross a wide avenue. The fort is 100–200 meters away, you can see very clearly the gunmen's positions in the mist. I'm nervous but it seems we don't have a choice. In fact yes, Abu Bilal had us cross just to show us, so we have to cross back again. Our annoyance makes him laugh.

A car is finally found and six of us pile in, with 'Umar and Abu 'Adnan who has turned up with our things. At an FSA checkpoint, we also take on a guy with an AK, Abu Jafar: Bab Drib isn't very safe, the Alawite neighborhoods and the *shabbiha* aren't far. We weave through the little streets, then cross two *shawari al-mout* at top speed, murmuring "*Bismillahi ar-Rahman ar-Rahim.*" At the entrance to Bab Drib, an FSA checkpoint. Not far there is a school, where the sniper who killed the boy is posted. We find the street, but the child is already at the mosque. We go there on foot. There are FSA soldiers everywhere. The body is in the prayer hall in the basement, on a wooden bier, wrapped in a shroud, with plastic flowers around his head, surrounded by children and older people. Three children against a pillar are quietly crying. The body is uncovered to show us the wound, in the belly. The skin is already yellow, the eyes slightly open, his nostrils have been filled with cotton. He has the beginnings of a moustache, a light down. Filmed by Abu Bilal, 'Umar gives a brief, furious speech in front of the body.

The child's name was Muhammad N. and he was thirteen, not twelve. It's the father who tells us the story. He was breaking wood for the *sobia* in front of the house, last night around 11:00 PM. He had a little light and the sniper shot him. I ask if we can publish his name: "We've lost the dearest thing we had, it doesn't matter now."[43] The child didn't die right away, they tried to bring him to the clinic, he bled to death.

The father, surrounded by friends, dignified, is keeping everything in. Only his eyes, humid and swollen.

Their house is shot at all the time. Riddled with holes. The sniper also killed a mentally handicapped person, another child of fifteen, ten days ago.

On the phone of one of the people around us, video of the washing of the corpse of an older man, killed by a bullet to the head by another sniper. He was the brother of the man showing me the video. His eleven-year-old son, on a bike, got hit in the shoulder, he rushed to save him and the sniper shot him. Probably a *shabbiha*, the shooting came from the Alawite neighborhood of Nezha, from a checkpoint.

People press in around us. The stories pour out. A young guy shows us a big scar on his back. He had shouted *Allahu Akbar!* as he crossed a street and was hit by a bullet.

Another man: "We don't even dare take out the trash. After 4:00 PM, you can't set foot outside." He lives on the same street as the one where the boy was killed. This street is so dangerous that the man whose brother was killed opened a hole through the walls between his house and his brother's, as well as his neighbor's, to be able to visit them without going outside.

Another young man, from the same street, tells me his father was killed. It happened at a different place; he was

---

43   For reasons explained in the preliminary note, I am not publishing the child's full name, despite the permission given by his father.

coming home with some errands and was killed from the citadel. The door to this family's apartment is under fire from the sniper at the school, they also had to knock an opening in the back to go out.

This sniper also entertains himself by killing cats. He has already killed eight. There are about ninety soldiers in the school, sandbags at the windows, and the building is concrete. The sniper is safe.

Another kid shows us his hand, two fingers cut off by a bomb, and his belly, starred with little black dots, scars from one of the infamous nail bombs. He is thirteen.

Yet another kid, also thirteen, with nail bomb scars on his legs.

A man undresses, shows his chest crisscrossed with scars. He was bringing back bread and milk with his son. When he reached the checkpoint, he made a sign: "Wait, I'm crossing," and they shot him three times in the body. He rushed to the boy and pinned him to the ground, lying over him, still making the gesture: "Wait, wait." Some people ended up dragging him from the street with a stick.

The brother of the dead boy says goodbye to him, kisses him and caresses him gently, crying. He strokes his face with infinite tenderness. Then it's the father's turn, at the head of the bier, as the brother sobs on a relative's shoulder. Nearby, a man murmurs "*Allahu Akbar, Allahu Akbar, Al-Hamdulillah*," with fervor.

Many children around the coffin, young ones with red eyes. The windows to the prayer hall are filled with cinderblocks, to protect the faithful from the shooting.

Noon prayer. A young guy chases the kids around the bier: "Go pray." Afterwards, they'll bring the body in front of the *qibla* and they'll say the prayer for the dead. Then it will be brought to the cemetery and immediately buried. A dozen FSA soldiers will accompany us to protect us.

When the time comes, a crowd of youths and children crowd around the bier and lift it, chanting *La ilaha illallah*. It is set down in front of the *qibla*, the father and brother just in front, the rest of the faithful in a line. The imam recites a prayer repeated by the faithful: "There is no God but God." Then he comes over to the side of the congregation and leads the prayer. He repeats *Allahu Akbar*! but the prayer is silent. Then the faithful salute the angels and take the body away, chanting "*La ilaha . . .*"

In the street, small demonstration. Standing on a wall, young men cry out slogans as the bier is carried around in circles. Then the crowd sets off through the narrow streets, two young guys sitting on the shoulders of other youths lead the shouting, FSA soldiers fire in the air, with pistols first then with Kalashnikovs, a woman veiled in black watches, crying. Near the cemetery, the FSA escort separates from the crowd, a dozen men in uniform, with an RPG. Shots fired in the air, we slip between the graves, the mud sticks to the feet, the hole is ready, with cinderblocks on the bottom. Guns fired in the air, the body is lifted and placed in the ground, the brother weeps, the father is stiff against the wall, livid. A gravedigger surrounds and covers the body with cinder blocks. The father approaches and says a brief prayer for his son. Everyone goes out into the street, the family lines up, and the relatives and friend pass

by shaking their hands and embracing them. I join in. Then
Ra'id.

*The activists then propose to take us to see another atrocity, I
don't understand exactly what or where. But on the way the
plan goes haywire. This is how we'll find ourselves in the neighborhood of Karam al-Zaytun, south-west of the citadel, at the
edge of the Alawite neighborhoods.*

We leave, still seven in the car. Quick acceleration at certain
intersections. Then suddenly we veer into a street. We get
out. There's gunfire up ahead. Hesitation, then Ra'id starts
off at a run. I move up to the FSA checkpoint a little further
on, hugging the wall of the avenue where gunfire keeps ech-
oing, for about thirty meters. Then Abu Ja'far and 'Umar
lead the way and we run in the streets. There is a wounded
civilian, we're told. We arrive at a small clandestine clinic.
The man is lying in his blood on the operating table as they
give him first aid. He was hit by a bullet through the base of
the skull. He is still panting, spitting blood. They sit him up
so he can vomit blood as 'Umar barks out a speech for Abu
Bilal's camera. The boy, who looks very young, is semi-
conscious and rolls his eyes, his face covered in blood. He is
twitching and keeps vomiting blood. But the trajectory is
low in relation to the brain, maybe he has a chance? They
take him out on a stretcher and load him into a taxi which
starts off honking as gunfire rings out. It's still the same
shooter. The doctor says he might survive, *insha'Allah.*

The witness arrives, an older man in a camouflage jacket.
He's an FSA soldier who was at the checkpoint, near the

Sa'id ibn 'Aamir mosque. The young man arrived holding a bag full of medicine, for his parents, a transparent bag that we are shown. His identity card is inside. His name is 'Umar A. and he was born in 1985. He was crossing the street toward the FSA checkpoint and the security forces shot him.

Another urgent case arrives, no, two, an older man and a fat woman. Chaos. The woman was hit by a bullet in the jaw and looks at me with wide open eyes full of fear. They sit her up to bandage her. The wound is deep but doesn't seem fatal. The man is wounded in the left shoulder. He pants as they give him emergency care, rolls his eyes, clutches Ra'id's hand. Once the woman is bandaged, they lay her down on a stretcher to evacuate her. They have no material here to operate.

The man is still conscious, he is panting but doesn't complain, he is suffering. "This is nothing," says the doctor. "One guy came, he was nothing but meat. Lower down there was nothing left." Next to the wounded man, I squelch through blood.

Abu Bilal is holding his head, he looks as if he can't take any more.

The wounded man is loaded into the back of a small truck, with his IV drip. Another man lies down next to him. He must not be seen, otherwise the checkpoints would shoot again.

We go to talk with the doctor, at his home near the emergency center. Honking. Another case, but it's not too serious and we don't go back. It is 1:30 PM, all this happened in about 45 minutes.

Most of the wounded are ferried to the hospital in Bab as-Sba'a, where we were yesterday. But often there aren't any doctors there either. Otherwise they bring them to Inshaat, or elsewhere. In Bab as-Sba'a, the doctors are very worried. They can't keep the wounded. As soon as the operation is over, they send them back to their homes, still under anesthesia. No post-op.

The twenty-seven-year-old youth, 'Umar A., is dead, a man who has just come in tells us.

The doctor is actually a nurse practitioner, a *musa'id fani*. There are no more doctors in the neighborhood, he says. They all fled because of the systematic arrests of doctors. They go to protected places, to the countryside. "Doctors have been targeted since the beginning of the events," he explains, like all his colleagues. He carries a pistol on his belt.

A witness explains about the two victims. They were wounded separately. The woman was walking in front of the mosque, like 'Umar A., and the checkpoint (a mixed *shabbi-ha*-Security checkpoint) shot at her. An hour earlier a man was coming out of the mosque and was hit in the neck. He died at the health center, before we arrived. No one dares go to the mosque anymore, there's too much shooting, four people a day, no more. The first one killed was one of those.

The witness is from the neighborhood, a civilian.

As for the man wounded in the shoulder, he was hit at another place, one street away.

They explain: there is a succession of streets held by the *shabbiha*, with checkpoints at each one. They shoot at anything that moves in the line of fire, man, woman, child.

Discussion about food. The falafels we've been carrying around since the mosque, and which we haven't touched, are still in the car. The nurse practitioner sends out for something. It is 1:45 PM and we still haven't eaten anything.

Honking. Another wounded. We go. Too bad about the food.

Four wounded in fact. Three light. One severe, dies in front of my eyes, without my realizing it, with a shudder. Hit in the jaw and the side of the belly. Lies there in underwear soaked in blood, very young.

The old man from before is brought back, the one who was wounded in the shoulder. He is dead. The corpse of 'Umar A. is there too, lying on the floor. The third dead man is lain next to them as the nurses busy themselves around the three wounded. He wasn't killed by bullets, but by shrapnel, the round ball bearings of a nail bomb.

Abu 'Adnan is discreetly weeping in a corner, overwhelmed. The three others are also wounded by ball bearings, but at their extremities. They're OK. They're stitched up without anesthesia, the guys are stoic.

One of the wounded is a medical student. We try to talk, but a baby is brought in, wounded in the groin by a bullet that went straight through. The baby is crying. In fact it isn't too serious.

[*The situation is quickly getting very tense, and we begin to worry about an incursion by the security forces. We ask questions about this.*] The neighborhood is secured by the FSA, thirty soldiers. We are told there is no risk of an attack.

When you move you stumble over the corpses. It's very chaotic, there are people everywhere.

The student wounded in the leg, very calm, gives himself an injection in the thigh. He was taking care of wounded at another health center, a shell fell just in front. He went out to help the victims, a second shell fell, that's when he was wounded and the young man with his jaw split open was killed.

There is an attack. Chaos and shooting in the street. We go out.

Crowd. Furious commotion further on. We all run there, Ra'id in front, me with 'Umar and Abu Bilal, who's flipping out. Three, four streets further on, hysterical crowd. They're finishing lynching a *shabbiha* they caught. Some enraged guys prevent Ra'id from photographing. Confusion. "Go, go." We return to the clinic and our friends decide to evacuate the neighborhood. They put us in a pickup truck to take us to our car. Ra'id and I lie down, the others laugh and take the piss out of us. The truck drops us off at the FSA checkpoint. We have to go around it and run thirty meters along the wall on the avenue to get to the car. No choice in any case. With the car, same thing: we have to go up the avenue, for several hundred meters, with our back to the checkpoint that's firing. We pile in. Apparently, a car full of FSA is going to drive behind us to cover us. I don't even have room to bend over. *Bismillahi ar-Rahman ar-Rahim, La ilaha illallah*, we peel off. Long moment of solitude. Finally we veer to the left and the tension bursts out in laughter and howls: "*Takbir! Allahu Akbar!*"

We stop. A black pickup arrives with two FSA soldiers standing in the back, above a corpse. He's a massive man, naked under a blanket, covered in blood, lying on his belly, his head crushed and his tied arms dangling from the back of the pickup: obviously the lynched *shabbiha*. It looks as if his head was smashed in with rifle butts. All around people are howling "*Allahu Akbar!*" The FSA displays the body throughout the neighborhood, triumphal procession of bloody revenge.

We start up again. Several crossings of dangerous avenues. The guys want to bring us to see the buildings destroyed yesterday. But when we arrive other FSA soldiers tell us: no, we can't approach, it's too dangerous. Near an avenue, under the concrete floor of a building under construction, we take a break near a *sobia* to eat the falafel. I have a hard time swallowing but I force myself to chew a few mouthfuls. It is 2:45 PM and my thoughts are clear, lucid.

After the falafel, we are taken through little streets to see the collapsed building, an immense pile of rubble at the end of an alleyway, still smoking. Here we're in Bab Tadmur, another neighborhood of the old city. A few men are trying in vain to excavate, there seem to be more bodies under the rubble. They've already extracted thirteen dead. According to people in the neighborhood, the building collapsed under a rain of RPGs, but that hardly seems credible.

[*Notes taken later on that evening.*] After, we go back. It's not too complicated, there's just one last sniper avenue to cross. Just when we emerge, a taxi appears opposite, we have to make a big swerve. Then we pass. As soon as we're behind cover we all burst out yelling, "*La ilaha illallah,*" then "*Takbir – Allah Akbar!*" We shout like madmen, a brief release. Then we cross the neighborhood.

The guys still insist on showing us a mosque riddled with shrapnel. I'm exhausted, I've still eaten almost nothing, and someone orders me some *sfihas*, but before they're ready a small truck passes at top speed with a wounded man, we jump into the car to follow it, I badger Ra'id who like me can't bear any more: "Come on, journalist, back to work, come on! What will this one be, the jaw? Leg blown off? Belly ripped open?" Ra'id doesn't find this very funny. But the truck crosses the avenue to Bab as-Sba'a and we decide not to follow it. They drag us to one more house, to show us another wounded man, from earlier on, who had both his legs shot out from under him as he was working on his roof to fix something. I'm so exhausted I don't even have the strength to take off my boots, and I stay in the courtyard, sprawled on a chair. But heavy gunfire breaks out, quite close, so I take off my boots and go in. Ra'id photographs, the guy is lying on a sofa, both legs in casts. I don't take any notes. Then we go home. In the street, FSA soldiers are jogging in the opposite direction, some of them with RPGs. The shooting continues, it slaps into the walls above us, it's the soldiers from the citadel firing all around to terrorize the inhabitants. It will last for over an hour; and the crackle of Kalashnikovs will soon be joined by the more sustained hammering of machine guns. A little later Abu Layl will tell us that the FSA counter-attacked a checkpoint that had shot at civilians, and killed two soldiers.

Reaching home I feel absolutely spent, washed out, drained of all energy. I piss, wash my hands and face, and brush my teeth with a brush and toothpaste bought in the street. I didn't have time to do it this morning.

Afterwards, pretty quickly, they serve us food, an omelet, some *labneh*, and some halvah. It's delicious and it fixes us up. The activists are already working, I start to as well. As soon as we got back to the house, they rushed to their laptops and began working, four guys in all facing each other around the table. Videos are downloaded, edited, and uploaded to YouTube in under an hour. Links multiply on Facebook, on all the revolutionary pages. A little later, Abu Bilal gives a live interview on Orient TV, by telephone.

Abu Layl has brought a big laminated sheet with a Google Earth photo of the zone that goes from the Citadel to Sittine Street (Sixty Street). The snipers who were shooting at the Sa'id ibn 'Aamir mosque are in Wadi al-Dhahab, an Alawite neighborhood. North of the zone, where there are the *shabbiha* posts that fire street after street, is Zahra. This morning, we passed those streets driving along the al-Jala swimming pool, behind the big cemetery of Bab Drib. The kid was buried in the little cemetery, on the other side of the avenue.

Information pours in. After our departure from Karam al-Zaytun, the Army fired shells at four houses, causing, for now, three deaths and about fifty wounded. Then the *mukhabarat* and the *shabbiha* penetrated the neighborhood, entering houses and arresting people. They attack by shooting indiscriminately, then advance with BTRs, the FSA can't withstand them. According to ʻUmar, who reached a contact over there on the phone, they entered a house and shot an entire family, twelve people. The *shabbiha* have been threatening people in that neighborhood for three days so they'll leave, because the *shabbiha* want to set up posts in the houses. They handed out pamphlets ordering people to leave. The attack and massacre today is following up on that.

According to the TV, al-Qusayr is being bombed. It could be complicated getting out.

7:00 PM. Some FSA groups leave the neighborhood to reinforce Karam al-Zaytun. On YouTube, an activist from over there has already posted a film of the massacre: on a bed, four bloodied little children, one seemingly an infant, a fifth one on the floor, one eye exploded, not even ten yet, a young woman still veiled, maybe the mother, other bodies. Everyone looks, we play it over and over again.

Abu Layl comes in and proposes we go back to Karam al-Zaytun to see the bodies. I'm too nervously exhausted to stand up, much less go out again, but Ra'id shakes himself, gets up and says: "*Yallah*." None of the activists want to go and Abu Layl bawls them out: "The foreigner is going and you won't? Aren't you ashamed?" Finally one of them agrees and they leave.

8:00 PM. The mosques start up the *takbir*. I don't know what this means. We can hear "*Allahu Akbar*" sung in chorus, interrupted by gunfire.

The FSA does not return fire coming from the citadel. It's pointless and it wastes ammunition.

According to the latest news, the children in the house had their throats slit, and "*'Ali*" written on their chests. If it's true, it's a deliberate attempt to provoke a sectarian war. But to be checked.

9:00 PM. The shooting resumes. Abu Bilal gives an interview by Skype.

9:15 PM. Return of Ra'id. Three of the children had their throats slit, the others were executed point blank with a bullet in the head. Two children survived: 'Ali, a three-year-old boy, and Ghazal, a little four-month-old girl, wounded by a bullet. Two adults in the family also survived, they were at work when it happened. [*The bodies, along with the two surviving children, had been brought to the health center in Karam al-Zaytun where we were earlier, and that's where Ra'id saw them. Contrary to the information received, there was no "Shiite signature" on the corpses.*]

When Ra'id arrived there, the baby was babbling, but the three-year-old boy was in tears, terrorized, no one could calm him down. I saw it later on YouTube, it's even worse than the deaths. In any case it's always worse for the survivors than for the dead, the dead don't feel anything anymore.

The victims belong to an extended family that lived in two adjoining houses. Sunni, but they lived on a mostly Alawite street. The massacre didn't occur in Karam al-Zaytun, as we thought, but in Nasihin, around 3:30 PM. They show us exactly where on the printed Google Earth photo: it's on a street south of the Bab Drib mosque where we went to the boy's funeral this morning. Beyond the avenue lies an Alawite neighborhood; the apartment blocks west of the street are also Alawite.

There are three eyewitnesses, neighbors who saw the killers arrive in BTRs, wearing military uniforms and headbands, black on yellow, with the slogan "*Ya 'Ali!*" – Shiites, then, if it's true. It could also be a provocation, to intensify the hatred between the communities. The witnesses claim that they saw, through a hole in the wall of their house, the end of the massacre: seven killers, busy murdering the children. When the killers left, the checkpoint at the end of the street began firing to cover their escape.

Ra'id spoke to one of the witnesses, a man of fifty or sixty. He doesn't rule out that the man didn't actually see the events. The corpses, however, are irrefutable.

As this man's testimony seemed rather incoherent and only partly credible, we left out most of his information from the articles published in Le Monde, *including the detail about the "Shiite" headband.*

10:00 PM. Al Jazeera claims that the FSA in Baba 'Amr captured five Iranian officers, working as snipers. The TV shows the five men, dressed in black, bearded, with an unreadable identity card. We're going to call them to check, and ask if we can see them.

It would appear clearly, a week later, that this video was a piece of disinformation, organized, it seems, by 'Abd ar-Razzaq Tlass. The five men were indeed Iranians, but engineers working at the Homs power plant, captured by the FSA. The identity cards supposed to identify them as pasdarans were in fact their certificates of discharge from military service. Le Monde published a detailed article about this affair on February 2, written by Christophe Ayad.

The gunfire resumes, heavier and more sustained than ever. Several explosions, one after the other. Noise like fireworks.

According to Abu Bilal, it's al-Bayada and al-Khalidiya that are being bombed. Explosions closer, Bab as-Sba'a probably. The activists are in contact with each other through a real-time online network, and exchange information between neighborhoods.

The shooting doesn't stop. Long sustained hammering, an AA gun probably, and shells, with an constant noise now of Kalashnikovs and machine guns.

Abu 'Adnan tells us it's the FSA attacking the main police station, in the center, as well as the checkpoints between Bab Drib and Karam al-Zaytun. They also destroyed a BRDM[44] on Cairo Street.

10:45 PM. The shooting and bombing continues without pause. The loudspeakers of the local mosque start howling *"Allahu Akbar."* In the street, dozens of voices chant *"La ilaha illallah!"* and *"Allahu Akbar!"* They draw closer, then move away.

Ra'id, who had gone to the FSA checkpoint, returns: "There's shooting everywhere. This isn't skirmishes, it's war."

---

44   *Boyevaya Razvedyvatelnaya Dozornaya Mashina,* "Combat Reconnaissance Patrol Vehicle," a Soviet armored vehicle on four wheels, amphibious and lightly armored, with a turret usually armed with a 14.5 mm machine gun.

Friday, January 27

Safsafi – Bab Drib – Safsafi

10:00 AM. Awakening. The guys are sleeping everywhere around me, on little mattresses on the floor; 'Umar Talawi has been sleeping for fourteen hours almost without moving. It rained for much of the night but finally it stopped. It's calm. There's no gunfire. Outside everything is sodden, you can hear a few shots in the distance, that's all. It starts raining again.

Noon, time for the Friday demonstrations. The activists separate: 'Umar goes to Bab as-Sba'a, Abu Bilal takes us to Bab Drib, with Mahmud, to the Hanableh mosque where we stopped yesterday to order the *sfihas* we never got to eat. The people in the neighborhood are organizing a new demonstration, and the activists will broadcast it live on Al Jazeera to support them. In front of the mosque, the trees are covered with an immense revolutionary flag, black-white-green with red stars. We came on foot, in the rain, it's not far from where we're staying. When we arrive, it's the call to prayer; in a shop opposite the mosque, caged canaries of all colors trill and sing in chorus with the imam.

The mosque fills up, it's the sermon. The imam stresses the cooperation people should show to each other. We must come to the aid of those who are suffering. He recalls the tradition of the Prophet and his companions, who sacrificed themselves to come to the aid of those who were suffering. Abu Bakr gave his entire fortune to the needy. The tone rises, takes on shrill, hysterical accents. The crowd cries out in chorus *"Allahu Akbar!"* The imam talks about all the blood that's been shed in the neighborhood: "It's our blood, all these souls killed are our children. But even so, we say to all our oppressors, to all our tyrants, to all those who have succumbed to hubris: Whatever you do, victory will be ours."

When you witness this noon Friday prayer, you're struck by how much the ritual serves to bring together and unite the community. This is where the collective will is formed and takes shape, focused by the sermon. Unlike Christian prayer in Europe, attended by only a handful of the faithful, here the entire neighborhood takes part, adults and children – the men in any case, meaning the ones who make the decisions concerning the collectivity. It's truly a mechanism for forming a "public opinion," in which even those who don't agree, or who don't come to pray, take part in one way or another. It's thanks to such mechanisms that one can speak of "collective will."

End of prayer. As usual, a great collective cry – *"La ilaha illallah!"* – repeated by everyone, as the faithful pour out of the mosque as they fluidly slip on their shoes, without stumbling (not the case for me). The demonstration forms.

I cross the street and try to take a picture from a fruit seller's stall. Immediately I'm set upon by two older, moustached men, in their forties. I just barely manage to put away my camera and take out my cellphone to call Ra'id, so he can come explain, all the while repeating "*Sahafi fransawi, sahafi fransawi,*"[45] two of the few words I know. Immediately one of the moustached guys, howling, tears away my cellphone and grabs my wrist. People start shouting, I try to catch Ra'id's attention, he's photographing a little further away, finally he comes. More arguing, the guy won't have any of it, Ra'id is more or less held too. Someone calls over a bearded soldier who asks questions, Ra'id looks for Abu Bilal, explaining we're with him. Finally an activist recognizes us and signals them that it's OK. The soldier hands me back my cellphone and apologizes.

A man takes me into a building still under construction, but already partially inhabited, to get a view from above. The rain has finally stopped and the sun is peeking out through the clouds. It's the same joyful ritual, the people lined up in the street in front of the mosque, the same songs, the same slogans, with a few new ones:

"O my mother, they slit the children's throats with their own hands!" [*Allusion to the Nasihin massacre the day before.*]

"The people demand capital punishment for the butcher!"

"The people demand the militarization of the revolution!"

---

45   "French journalist."

Under the leader, men unfurl the banners printed by our French-speaking friend. This Friday is the one for the right to self-defense.

One of the youths, in the demonstration, is waving a Turkish flag. "Why?" I ask Abu Bilal – "They don't have any others!"

Passage behind the demonstration of a dozen FSA soldiers, in camouflage uniforms, three even with helmets. Immediately the crowd starts chanting "Long Live the Free Army!" The kids run after them and swarm around them. I join them, at the corner, near the FSA checkpoint. The officers have piled into a big black 4×4, and three soldiers are standing on the rear bumper. There is a *ra'ed*, a *naqib*, and a *mula ̧im awwal*. They tell Ra'id that they've come to protect the demonstration, but maybe they've also come to show themselves. A kid shouts to his father: "It's them, it's them, it's the Free Army!" Slowly they head toward the demonstration, and enter the crowd to the shouts of "Allah grant long life to the Free Army!" Procession, three soldiers standing on the roof, then they move forward and leave. All of a sudden the rain starts falling and the demonstration comes to an end.

The FSA men come back and an old guy on a motorbike empties his clip into the air, laughing. Then a little further on an Army post starts firing.

Apparently, yesterday, the FSA gave a pounding to the Zahra checkpoint from where the men who massacred the family had come. If the FSA show themselves in force today, it's probably also to reassure the population. The 4×4 with the officers continues to come and go after the demonstration. And the people are clearly happy to see them, and to see us as well (paranoid fits aside). For many Syrians, our presence seems as much a sign of moral support as the promise of reliable information reaching the outside world.

I go pick up some apples and mandarin oranges at the fruit seller. He's one of the men who held me earlier on, and he doesn't let me pay. Return under the rain. Near the house, a mouthwatering smell draws me to a kebab seller. Eleven days in Syria and I haven't eaten a single kebab. We order a kilo, for all the guys, which the vendor's son will bring us in an hour.

At the house, Anjad, back from Bab as-Sba'a. Three wounded, one seriously, with a bullet that went through both legs. The shooting has resumed from the citadel. Nonetheless, for a Friday, it seems calm.

Yesterday the FSA attacked three places: checkpoints in Zahra, checkpoints on the Damascus road, at the entrance to the al-Midan neighborhood, and Military Security on Hajj Aatef square, inside al-Midan. They apparently entered the Security building. In the neighborhoods they took numerous checkpoints, killed the soldiers, captured the weapons and ammunition, and withdrew. They can't hold these positions in front of armor. The operations were led by the guys from Baba 'Amr, the al-Faruk *katiba*.

In principle, according to Anjad, the FSA tries not to kill the Army soldiers who surrender and to capture the officers, including *mukhabarat*. But they systematically execute the *shabbiha*.

Video of the demonstration in Bab as-Sba'a. They burn a portrait of Putin with one of Bashar. The demonstrators hit them with their shoes.

The kebabs finally arrive. We lay a tablecloth on the floor and everyone crowds around, even Abu al-Hakam, the boy who always serves us tea. Delicious.

———

4:00 PM. We go out. Extraordinary light, the sun pierces through the clouds and illuminates sections of buildings while it still rains. It's calm, kids are playing in the street. We meet a bearded soldier, a policeman who defected because of the regime's exactions: "Yesterday's massacre is an example of why we're fighting." His eleven-year-old kid carries his Kalashnikov.

Beautiful long stroll through the neighborhood. The light keeps changing as the clouds go by. The puddles reflect the sky and the fronts of the buildings. There are a few isolated shots, a few explosions, but overall it's calm. On a square where children are playing, we chat with some FSA soldiers. One of them takes us a little further off, to a building under construction which we enter by climbing a wall. We climb to the roof, carefully: the openings in the stairwell look out on to the citadel nearby, no more than 200 meters away. We look at it out of the corner of our eye, a vast mass of earth covered with green, brilliant grass, with fragments of walls, surmounted by an immense Syrian flag that I photograph stealthily: no point getting shot for Assad's flag, Ra'id jokes. The stroll continues, we meet some inhabitants, FSA soldiers. The neighborhood visited this way seems tiny, you can't go 500 meters without bumping into an avenue controlled by a checkpoint, a line of fire.

We visit the street that leads to Bab as-Sba'a, the one with the tires at the end, which we had rushed down the other night. Several cars pass at top speed toward Bab as-Sba'a, without getting shot at. The perpendicular street offers a line of fire to the citadel, you have to walk hugging the wall and watch out. We return calmly.

Le Monde has printed our material from yesterday on page three, with a headline on the front page and the photo taken by Ra'id. They ask him for more info to print more material tomorrow on the massacre.

Later that night Ra'id would write a long piece about his nighttime crossing of the city, the previous night, which would be published in Le Monde *dated Sunday, January 29–Monday, January 30, with one of his photos of the eleven bodies of the massacred family. On Saturday the 28th,* Le Monde *had already published a first photo, with an unsigned article written in Paris on the basis of information I had sent them by e-mail.*

Big argument between the activists. Anjad throws his camera and telephone on the table. 'Umar Talawi was criticizing him for his captioning of the YouTube videos from the day before. Apparently an ambiguous phrase had made a lot of people think 'Umar was dead.

Shower at Anjad's place. Posh building, just next to the house where we're staying (which is much less so, posh I mean), with plants in the marble staircase; bourgeois apartment, with elegant furniture, impeccably clean, good-quality rugs. The father receives me in the living room, near the stove (the radiators – they have them here, a rare thing – aren't working, they consume too much diesel fuel). He lived for a long time in Brussels but only remembers a few words of English. The shower, the first one since Baba 'Amr, is a magnificent moment. Ra'id arrives afterwards for his, and we drink tea. When we leave, Anjad taps his fingernail on the living room door, to warn the women, whom we never see. Even the bourgeois maintain *purdah*.

The father offers me a very beautiful rosary made of blue stone. In Arabic one says *misbaha*, from the word *subhan* which you mouth when you count your beads: *Subhan Allah*, "praise to God." The Persian word I've always used, *tasbeh*, is formed from the same root.

———

2:30 AM. I still can't get to sleep. In the big room in front, the room for the FSA soldiers, there's been singing for hours. I get up and go see. About twenty men are sitting all around against the wall, smoking cigarettes and drinking tea or maté, and taking turns singing, a cappella. I don't understand the words, of course, but they sound like love songs, maybe also songs about the city. The voices tremble, groan, sigh, when one finishes, another starts up. One man especially leads the singing, a man in his forties, with a narrow face, bearded, slightly reddish hair, cunning eyes, completely toothless except for a single incisor in the lower jaw. He sings with intense, concentrated emotion, and seems to know all the songs asked of him. When he pauses, another one takes it up. The others listen, call out, sometimes clap their hands. No one interrupts anyone, there's no contest or competition, everyone sings for the pleasure of singing and listens for the pleasure of listening, all together.

Saturday, January 28

Safsafi – Baba 'Amr – al-Khalidiya – al-Bayada

It had been decided, with the editorial board of Le Monde, *that these ten days in Homs were enough for the articles, and that it was time I go back to Lebanon, while Ra'id, as initially planned, would stay a little longer. The day before, Ra'id had telephoned the FSA in Baba 'Amr, and it had been agreed that we'd come this morning so that Ibn Pedro could exfiltrate me into Lebanon. For various reasons, as will be seen, it did not work that day, or the following days; I would only finally manage to leave on Thursday, February 2.*

Morning. Early awakening for departure to Baba 'Amr and, *insha'Allah*, further with Ibn Pedro. In the courtyard, a pensive, melancholic soldier is smoking a cigarette, seated. Two comrades join him. Noise of weapons being dismantled mixed with bits of song. As they make tea another soldier arrives, pushing his electric bicycle. He shows us a long, twisted metal tube, a piece of a small rocket, which fell this morning in Karam al-Zaytun. Two dead.

8:30 AM. A young taxi driver sent by Abu 'Adnan comes to pick us up. We leave by the little streets of Safsafi and then, instead of continuing on via the souk, as we did on the way in, we emerge, to my great surprise, on to the avenue that circles the citadel, just at the foot of the mound. Raising my head, I see very clearly the shooting positions, surrounded with sandbags, just above us. It doesn't seem to bother the driver, who slips into a wide avenue toward the center. There's a little traffic, everything looks normal. We pass not far from the military security building, through a neighborhood, take another avenue; at an intersection, in front of the Education Ministry, the driver makes a U-turn just in front of three soldiers on guard duty, who royally ignore us. Then it's Insha'at, crossing Brazil Street, and the first FSA checkpoints which stop us: "Who are you?" – "French journalists." A little surprised but not troublesome, they let us pass.

We find Hassan's apartment where we wake up Ahmad, still the bear. Long wait. Ibn Pedro arrives around 10:15 AM. The conversation is quick. Today, he's only going to the town where we stopped on the way here, then he's returning to Baba 'Amr; he could hand me over to someone else to take me to al-Qusayr, but it's not safe. What's more, Fury forgot his cellphone in Tripoli and can't be reached. On the other hand, in two days he can do a round trip directly for al-Qusayr, just to take me there. We discuss briefly with Ra'id, then opt for that solution. So, return to al-Khalidiya and al-Bayada.

———

Breakfast sitting on a bench in the sun, on the central square of Khalidiya. A moment of grace. Warm pastry stuffed with walnuts and honey, bought at the "*Pâtisserie Abu Yaser*" [*sic*] whose sign is in French, and a kind of drink made from warm cream and ground nuts, rather cloying. Afterwards, we go to the barber to get shaved, but he's still closed. His neighbors, in a machine repair shop, invite us over for coffee. According to them, the shelling on Thursday night [*the one we had heard from Safsafi*] didn't cause any victims in the environs of the square, although a house was hit by a mortar shell; further on, they don't know. It is 11:15 AM.

Ra'id, last night, also went to see the singers after I finally went to sleep. Abu Layl and one of his friends were singing quatrains by 'Umar Khayyam, in a version by Umm Kulthum. Ra'id sang a little with them. *Tarab*, the emotion you feel listening to music.

The coughing fits keep worsening from day to day. They undo me completely, leave me empty and trembling for a long moment.

Gunfire volleys as we drink coffee. The shooting is from a building next to the al-Katib cemetery, in a street in Khalidiya. At that point we hear shouting. A funeral procession emerges, men carrying a bier, chanting "*La ilaha illallah!*" surrounded by armed men shooting in the air. The dead man on the bier isn't visible beneath the plastic flowers. He was killed by a sniper. The procession heads for the mosque, in the crackling of gunfire. I go back to finish my coffee as Ra'id runs after it to photograph it.

The funeral processions I've seen here don't express mourning or contemplation, but rage and the live pain of loss.

The crowd has stopped a little further on, at the mosque, and I head there with a kid who shows me the impact of Thursday's mortar shell, in a top floor apartment looking out on to the square. Ra'id is already in the mosque. The bier is set in a corner, surrounded by distraught people and onlookers. Two men in tears, probably a brother and the father. The victim is a handsome young man, solid, vigorous, transformed by death into a yellowish wax doll. Ra'id introduces me to Abu Bakr, an activist from the neighborhood he knew before. Abu Bakr explains that the man was killed by a sniper this morning at 8:00 AM, as he was going to work. He shows us the videos he took, the bloody body with its torso pierced by the bullet, the mother and sister shaking it, incredulous, overwhelmed with hysterical mourning.

The moment of grace didn't last long.

Ra'id stays to photograph the prayer and the burial. I go back to the machine shop. The barber where I want to get shaved is still not open. So I head back to the mosque. The prayer is about to end – the sermon for the dead, according to Ra'id, was overwhelming: "The imam really brought the faithful to the gates [*of Paradise*]" – and the people are getting ready to bear the dead body out. A young man is hoisted on to someone's shoulders and, hand raised, launches the first of the invocations: "*La ilaha illallah!*" Then the invocations follow each other, bawled out loudly by the faithful, as the leader waves a handsome framed portrait of the dead man, made in a photo studio and probably taken from the wall of his house. "To Paradise, by the millions, we will go as martyrs!" Then the procession leaves along the square, followed by FSA soldiers who fire long Kalashnikov volleys in the air. Kids rush between the feet of the marchers to pick up the casings, still burning hot. "We are all martyrs! All!" howls the leader, meaning dead men on probation. The procession moves around the square to the replica of the Old Clock, where they carry the bier around in circles, to the sound of invocations. The cemetery is five kilometers away, only two or three people will be able to accompany the remains, it's too dangerous. The barber is finally open and I can get my cheeks and neck shaved. I've got used to the goatee, it will serve for a few more days.

In front of the barber's, brief exchange with a very expressive young boy. "*Shahid*: Ahmad." He explains: "*Kannas*," and mimes a bullet in the back of the head and one through the chest. "*Uma shahid*," and with his hands he mimes the tears running down the face of the martyr's mother. "*Haram*,"[46] he concludes sadly.

In Syrian dialect, *kannas*, "sniper," is pronounced *gennas*. Plural *kannasa*.

Discussion on the square with Marcel Mettlesicfcn, a German journalist, half Colombian. He's here with a tourist visa, for the fourth time. We exchange information and contact details.

---

46   "Forbidden, illicit."

Marcel, who doesn't speak Arabic, was accompanied and helped by a young, friendly Syrian who introduced himself to us under the name 'Umar. I talked a little with him that day, and took down his contact details, as he said he was ready to work with any journalist who came to Homs, and several friends were asking me for contacts. But he was killed, coming to the aid of the wounded, during the great bombing of Khalidiya on the night of February 3. It was only then that I learned his real name, Mazhar Tayara, twenty-four years old.

I go to get some kebabs, liver for a change, as Ra'id waits his turn to get shaved. It's still as nice out. Further on, beyond the citadel probably, we hear explosions.

The kebabs take half an hour instead of the ten minutes promised, but are delicious. Ra'id is shaved and Abu 'Adnan joins us. Sitting in the sun, I drink a coffee and smoke a cigarillo as Abu 'Adnan organizes transport.

———

We cross from al-Khalidiya to al-Bayada in a small Suzuki truck, with Abu Bakr in a very good mood. To reach Abu Brahim's place, through a labyrinth of narrow streets, you have to cross four sniper avenues or streets. The last one is apparently the most dangerous. "This is where all the *sha-hids* of the neighborhood died," says the driver. But today the snipers aren't working much, it seems, and we cross without trouble, with passersby and children.

At the home of Abu Brahim in al-Bayada, finally.

Abu Brahim, a Sufi shaykh responsible for humanitarian aid for the neighborhood of al-Bayada, is Mani's contact who had organized our passage from Lebanon. Fadwa Suleiman, the Alawite actress who went over to the opposition, and who is often presented as the muse of the Syrian revolution, had been living at his place for months, and I had hoped to be able to meet her. But she had left for Zabadani, to support the people there who for some time had been resisting a bitter siege and bombardments.

Conversation. Rumors of an imminent attack? Abu Brahim doesn't think so. If there were concentrations of troops, he would know. It's always possible, but probably not for tomorrow.

As for the snipers, they continue to shoot. This afternoon, sustained fire, a little earlier, but no wounded. Yesterday three wounded. The FSA here doesn't have enough means, in men or ammunition, to counterattack.

A new *katiba* has been formed in the suburbs of Damascus, the Hussein ibn 'Ali *katiba*, a curiously Shiite reference. Abu Brahim: "No, we insist, Hussein is also our son [*for the Sunnis*]. This indicates that we don't have sectarian views."

Other *katibas* operational in Damascus and the far suburbs: the Abu 'Ubaydah ibn al-Jarrah *katiba*, the al-Hassan *katiba*, and the Qawafil ash-Shuhada ("Caravans of the Martyrs") *katiba*. The Hussein ibn 'Ali *katiba* has regiments in Damascus, Homs, Hama, Dara'a, and soon, "*in'sha'Allah*," in ar-Raqqah, 200 kilometers east of Hama.

Abu 'Umar, a neighborhood activist who has joined us: "Bashar al-Assad hasn't left us any other options but armed conflict. Demonstrations, dialogue, congresses, nothing worked. They only replied with bullets. They leave us no other choice."

Comment by Abu Brahim on Thursday's massacre: "It's a form of ethnic cleansing."

———

We go back out. The sniper street is twenty meters away from Abu Brahim's. There are snipers to the left and the right. "*Now not shooting. But ready. Not know when shooting,*" Abu 'Umar explains to me in rudimentary English. He shows me a Suzuki pickup riddled with holes: "*My friend killed in this car.*" Just here at the intersection. Targeted because he was transporting wounded.

Evening walk through the neighborhood. Muddy streets, rarely paved, and in the open spaces immense piles of garbage in bags, piled up for months and torn open. Many buildings under construction. Working-class neighborhood, poor, proletarian. In the streets, clusters of children follow us chanting anti-Bashar slogans. Little by little, the people are cutting down the olive trees planted in front of their houses to warm themselves; three girls, in front of a door, are struggling to saw through a trunk. At the windows, veiled girls spy on us, whispering. In a place with bare concrete walls, some youths are playing billiards. At the end, a broad four-lane avenue turned into a *shari 'al-mout*, a "street of death." We approach the corner carefully. Gunshots ring out regularly; Abu 'Umar forbids some youths who want to get to the other side from crossing. Last Thursday, five deaths at different crossings: three in the head, one in the neck, one straight through the chest. On a parallel street, a very long metal rod, with two hooks soldered at the end, lies on the ground: it serves to recover the wounded – and the dead – shot in the middle of the avenue. Abu 'Umar's apartment looks out on to the avenue from an upper floor. The walls on the sniper side are pierced by explosive bullets, and he was forced to move to the lower, more protected floor. By zooming through one of the holes, I can photograph the red sandbags, at the corner of a big intersection, from where the sniper is shooting. On the avenue, you can see big black traces with rusted wires, truck tires burned so that the smoke can cover people crossing.

A little further on, in another parallel street, we see some vehicles cross, a family in a Suzuki pickup, a taxi, a KIA with some FSA soldiers. They're not very visible in the neighborhood: their presence is weak, and the ones who are here don't show themselves much; the FSA checkpoint near Abu Brahim's is deserted. At each passage of a car, the sniper fires, but always two or three seconds too late. A taxi arrives on our side: we explain to him, he gives up and does a U-turn. In front of a dried fruit and candy store where we stop to buy some almonds, a crowd of young people surrounds us. A very handsome boy, in a blue tracksuit, shouts at Ra'id: "They arrested my father, they arrested my brother, they beat my mother! They came to arrest me, and if they find me, they'll kill me! All that because I go out and say I don't like Bashar!" He stretches out his neck and pinches his Adam's apple: "My only weapon is my voice." He is a demonstration leader, he's seventeen, and in front of us he performs a demonstration of his art, arm outstretched, accompanied by a little drum, starting up chants that all the kids swarming around us take up in chorus.

On the way back, we pass a house that is flying, rather incongruously, next to the flag of a soccer team, a "governmental" Syrian flag. The owner can't be blamed for it: he was killed by a sniper, two months ago. A little further on there's an old Hajj sitting on a chair, smoking in the company of a friend, who tells us how he was tortured for twenty-one days by the *mukhabarat*, beaten, electrocuted, accused of complicity with terrorism, him, a sick old man. At each stop some people gather, try to tell their stories.

A few words about our host, Abu Brahim. Before the events he was a truck driver, with just some religious knowledge; today he's a local authority, widely respected in his neighborhood, who manages humanitarian distributions for al-Bayada from the ground floor of his building. He's a Sufi, a Qadiri of the Shadhili branch; his first master was a Tunisian shaykh who died ten years ago, then a Syrian shaykh, member of the fatwa committee of the Umayyad mosque, Muhammad Abu al-Huda al-Yaqoubi. This shaykh had to leave the country after denouncing the repression ("It's a sin to kill people in this way") and entering into conflict with the mufti of Syria, Ahmad Badreddin Hassoun. "He is not the mufti of Syria," Abu 'Umar specifies. "He is the mufti of the regime, the mufti of Bashar."

With his shaved head, his great beard standing out from his chin, and his cunning smile, Abu Brahim could easily be taken for a Chechen. The comparison seems to please him.

Just like the Qadiriyya, a Sufi order founded by Abd al-Qadir al-Jilani in Baghdad in the twelfth century, the Naqshbandiyya is a branch of Sufism, founded in Bukhara in the fourteenth century by Bahauddin Naqshband al-Bukhari. I visited his tomb in 1998, and this is what I then discuss with Abu Brahim.

Spiritual conversation about the Naqshbandi and the tomb of Naqshband. Abu Brahim agrees that a pilgrimage to the tomb of Naqshband has value – not the mechanical value of a half-pilgrimage to Mecca, as the Uzbeks claim, but a spiritual value if the pilgrim goes to the saint's tomb to study his thought and to evolve spiritually. It's the same for Mecca: if you go there like an object, like your pair of shoes or your camera, and you return unchanged, there's no point.

He says there are a lot of Naqshbandi in Syria. There was a Naqshbandi shaykh in Ifrine, Hussein Qorqo, now dead, who was a friend of Al-Daghestani in Cyprus, a shaykh I know by reputation thanks to Misha Roshchin who had spent some time with him.

How Abu Brahim defines Sufism: "Being in balance between your inner and outer being, between the *batin* and the *zhahir*. *Zhahir* is appearance, the exoteric path, *batin* is the interior or the esoteric way. They are also two of the ninety-nine names of God."

———

Abu Brahim also has on his computer some videos of the lost Belgian, Pierre Piccinin. Sitting in this same living room, looking out of his depth and a little frightened, making phone calls to friends in Belgium, all on voicemail. Five hours before he showed up in a big brand new American car, a Ford or Chevrolet rented in Damascus, speaking not a word of Arabic, there had been a big battle between the FSA and the Army just where he passed through. "That man, God loves very much," says Abu Brahim. Then: "We welcomed him, we fed him, we sheltered him, and we filmed him. We told him: 'If you go back to see the regime and you say we mistreated you, we'll put the videos on YouTube.'" They were convinced he was sent by the regime. Photos of him here with Fadwa Suleiman, the Alawite actress.

Ra'id tries to call him. A little later, Mr. Piccinin calls back. He's actually an academic, a professor of political science and history. "I'm a specialist of the Arab-Muslim world. I don't speak Arabic but I get by very well with English." His line: "The SOHR[47] just tells lies, *Le Monde* too. I came there to see what was really going on because I don't believe the discourse of the media or the activists. They claimed there was bombing and I looked for the neighborhood. But I didn't see anything. I wrote objective articles about the situation, that's how I obtained my second visa. Of course I was supervised."

It continues for a while in this vein until in the end Ra'id, exasperated, retorts, "Sir, I'd like to advise you to change specialties. You speak English, specialize in the Anglo-Saxon world." He bawls him out pretty sharply, the guy equivocates, "We're not going to be polemical over the telephone," but of course doesn't listen. When Ra'id talks to him about the massacre and the article in *Le Monde*, he replies, "But

---

47 The Syrian Observatory for Human Rights, mentioned earlier.

who killed them?" To get here, Abu Brahim explains, he passed in front of all the snipers without noticing anything. In truth, there is a god for morons from Gembloux.

I was later able to take a look at Pierre Piccinin's production, on his blog. He presents a version of the events in Syria in complete conformity with the regime's propaganda, minimizing as much as possible the killings as well as the extent of the uprising. Neither his brief trip to Homs, without any translator and without any knowledge of the neighborhoods or the configuration of the city, nor his discussions with Abu Brahim and Fadwa Suleiman, will have changed his mind.[48]

---

48   *Note to the Verso edition*: Pierre Piccinin, in the months following the original French publication of this book, experienced his own abrupt "epiphany on the Road to Damascus." Having returned to Syria in April 2012 on a third government-sponsored trip, he somehow found himself arrested by regime forces and was detained in Homs, witnessing the hideous torture of his fellow Syrian prisoners and experiencing some mistreatment himself, before finally being released and expelled from the country. Over the following year, now fully converted to the cause of the rebellion, he returned repeatedly and clandestinely to Syria, with FSA units, and published two books about his experiences. On April 8, 2013, during his eighth trip, he was kidnapped in al-Qusayr together with the Italian reporter Domenico Quirico, possibly by Islamist elements of the al-Faruk *katiba*. Both men were released on September 8, 2013, reportedly after the Italian government paid a large ransom. This unpleasant experience seemed to have triggered a new conversion, and Pierre Piccinin caused something of a controversy by declaring that information overheard during his captivity proved that the regime was innocent of the August 21, 2013 Ghouta sarin gas massacre, a statement that Domenico Quirico categorically contradicts.

Sunday, January 29

Al-Bayada

Sunny morning. No more dreams for the past few days. The cough seems a little better after a cortisone injection made yesterday evening by Abu Hamza, the doctor.

Abu Hamza was one of Abu Brahim's many guests, to whom we didn't pay much attention until Ra'id asked Abu Brahim if he knew people who had been witnesses to torture: "Him," our host had replied, pointing to the doctor. Abu Hamza officiates in the little clandestine health center set up on the ground floor of Abu Brahim's building. Without any material or equipment, he can do almost nothing for his patients; out of frustration, he's thinking of abandoning medicine and taking up arms. "At night," he told me, "I spend hours picturing myself lying in ambush with a rifle and killing one of the snipers." He agreed to let me record his testimony, which he gave me half in English, half in Arabic, with a translation by Ra'id. I re-transcribe the interview here from the notes in my notebook rather than the recording.

Interview with Abu Hamza. Surgeon, worked at the military hospital since 2010. He was trying to obtain a new specialization, this is normal for a civilian doctor. The military hospital also took care of civilian patients: either in emergency care, or members of soldiers' families. The problems began with the revolution.

At first, he heard about strange things in the emergency room. When they brought in wounded demonstrators, their hands were tied and their eyes blindfolded. Abu Hamza wanted to see that with his own eyes and he went there: it was true. The first time he saw it, it was April [*2011*]. Military policemen, with male nurses, led the demonstrators to another room. Next to the emergency ward there are three rooms: a pharmacy, an X-ray room, and an intensive care unit. There the wounded, without any medical attention, were beaten with cables by those same military policemen and nurses. The victims were all men, sometimes fourteen- or fifteen-year-old boys, but not younger. Then they were taken to prison, without treatment. Several doctors took part in these tortures, whose names he took down.

Abu Hamzeh provided me with some of these names: since I cannot verify the information, I am not publishing them.

When the head doctor of the hospital – an Alawite from Tartus, a very good man – heard about this, he gave the order that patients not be beaten, and that they be given medical treatment. That was maybe twenty days after the beginning of the abuse. The result is that they treated them, then came to beat them at night in their beds.

"I treated a patient one day in the emergency room. The next day they brought him for an X-ray, with a cranial trauma he hadn't had the day before. That's how I discovered that they'd done something to him in the night. I asked a friend, a radiologist, for the details of the case, and he told me, 'He has a fracture of the skull, and cranial trauma, he's in intensive care now.' Two days later the patient died from this cranial trauma. He wouldn't have died from the wounds that I had treated the first day. He died from torture."

There was a room to keep the patients after treatment. The demonstrators were placed there, tied, their eyes blindfolded, and the catheter that helped them urinate was blocked; they were only given a quarter of a liter of water for six people, every other day, just a few drops to hydrate them.

When Abu Hamza would come in, the people begged him for water. The blocked catheter was causing lesions in their kidneys. "I saw two people fall into a coma because of that. One of them died. So I put a little camera in my pocket and went to film them. I entered the room to attend to patients. I was with a woman nurse, a sympathizer who helped me. There were no antibiotics, no serum, no medicine. I tried to unblock the catheters, but the bags of urine were full. I think they closed the catheters so the bags wouldn't burst, because they didn't change them. I emptied them and changed them. When I changed the bandages, I noticed a case of gangrene, and I told the orthopedic department about it, so the patient would receive antibiotics. Three days later I heard that this patient had been brought to the operating room and had

had his leg cut off above the knee. It was impossible for me to follow up on him.

"I filmed wounds, traces of beatings with cables. There were two torture tools: an electric cable and strips of reinforced rubber.

"I also went to the prison and spoke with three men. I took down their names to inform their families. One had a broken leg, another a bullet wound in the arm. They told me they were beaten and tortured in prison."

———

10:45 AM. Sudden interruption. Honking. A wounded man is being brought in. Everyone rushes to the emergency care center downstairs. Older man, in his fifties or sixties, with a bullet in the left side. Arm covered with tattoos, beautiful spirals, not a ritual tattoo, maybe a prison tattoo? Swift, precise, efficient gestures of Abu Hamza. The man is conscious and stoic, he is breathing heavily. Abu Hamza examines him, asks some questions. The bullet came back out, through the side of the flank. Abu Hamza doesn't know if the bullet went through the muscle or the abdomen. No instruments, he can't do an ultrasound scan, doesn't know if there's internal bleeding. If the abdomen is perforated, it's probably the ascending colon. He will have to be operated on, with a colostomy bag attached, and be stitched back up. If the man is not operated on he can die in two days, from peritonitis.

Search for someone with a portable ultrasound machine to come here. Abu Hamza gives some anti-tetanus injections and then antibiotics.

The man was shot by a sniper six streets from here, from the Nasser 'Ali school in al-Bayada. He was near his home. Sent his children back in and was shot. Another man was killed, from a bullet in the chest. The wounded man is perfectly conscious and speaks with Ra'id. "Fortunately the children weren't hit."

Tattoo: "Submission to my mother." Other beautiful designs, all hand-done. Scars also on the same arm, traces of self-mutilation with a razor.

Hardly a day without a death or a wounded person, whatever the neighborhood. I go back upstairs where it's warm. Breakfast is almost ready.

11:20 AM, we eat, another interruption, another wounded man. We go back down. It's the son of the first wounded man, a teenager about eighteen or twenty who caught a bullet through two fingers of his left hand. It's not too serious and we go back upstairs to eat as Abu Hamza bandages him.

Abu Brahim: "*Wallah*, we have been able to see that Israel is less harsh with the Palestinians than Arab governments with their own people. And the Israeli government would never do that to its own people." Ra'id doesn't entirely agree about the clemency of Israelis, especially in wartime.

An older gentleman joins us. He lives in Sabil, a mixed Sunni-Alawite neighborhood, mostly Alawite. He talks about the threats the Sunni inhabitants have received to force them to leave. Some had their houses burned down, others their cars. He lives at the corner of an intersection where there's a checkpoint and snipers on the roofs. They shoot at his house every day, he had to leave his apartment, too dangerous, but stayed in the building. His neighbors have got threats, ordering them to leave in twenty-four hours under pain of being killed or having their houses burned. He lives about 150 meters from the Alawites; all those living closer have already left; next to his place, all the Christians have moved away. "We've been living with them for forty years. They're our brothers. But they all had to leave, because of the constant shooting."

Four or five months ago, when his brother was wounded, he went to see his Alawite neighbors to remind them they were neighbors above all: "Whatever happens, whether the regime falls or stays, we'll remain neighbors, we'll continue to live together. Stop these military actions against us. Stop shooting at us."

The security forces armed the Alawite civilians, and some had been seen shooting from their houses. "They promised to stop doing it, but they haven't keep their word." The neighbor who came with him was arrested and held for one or two months.

———

1:00 PM. Interview with Abu Hamza, continued.

[*We pick up at the three prisoners in the cell.*] "One needed an emergency operation for his broken leg. They left him for three days, and finally brought him to our department with a severe fracture of the femur. The bone was jutting out. He wasn't like that when I saw him in the cell. In the end he was operated on by the orthopedic department.

"In the hospital, part of the staff wanted to help; but for others, it was the opposite. For example, a doctor who wanted to help a patient would say to the soldiers: 'Bring him to my department.' But the others would create new wounds, breaking more bones before bringing him there."

Even in the operating room, patients have their eyes blind-folded. The *mukhabarat* however don't come into the operating room, they wait outside. In exceptional cases, the *mukhabarat* designate a doctor, usually a military doctor, to watch over the patient, or else refuse him medical attention.

Another case he witnessed: some Air Force *mukhabarat* had confiscated two ambulances, and put two of their agents in each ambulance, disguised as nurses, but armed with Kalashnikovs. They went to the Homs cemetery. It was a Saturday; the day before, a dozen guys had been killed, and they were being buried that day. The Army began shooting at the people bringing the bodies to the funeral, from a checkpoint close to the cemetery. Then the *mukhabarat* arrived with the ambulances, pretending to come for the wounded, they opened the doors, took in the wounded and brought them to the military hospital. There, they didn't take them to the emergency ward but to the prison. It's a well-known story, the day of the massacre of the . . . cemetery (he can't remember the exact name).

Abu Hamza saw the ambulances return and bring the wounded directly to the prison. He recognized the Air Force *mukhabarat* by their special uniform and their white sneakers.

After this business, he was denied access to the prison and the surgery department, so he personally didn't see any more cases of torture or abuse. He worked at the military hospital until about twenty days ago: "In the morning I was supposed to treat soldiers, in the afternoon I treated revolutionaries. I couldn't take it anymore." For nine or ten months, he would come here to treat people secretly. He didn't feel at ease when he had to treat a *mukhabarat*; he didn't wish him any harm, but he didn't feel at ease, and preferred to stop. Over there, they have all the necessary material, here there's nothing. He feels his duty is here. He left everything, his house, his private clinic, the hospital. He officially resigned and that doesn't pose any problems.

Afterwards, he shows us the videos he filmed in secret, thanks to a camera-pen placed in the outer pocket of his lab coat. You can see the wounded very clearly, five in all, chained by their feet to the bed, naked under the sheets, their eyes blindfolded. The camera films the torture instruments, placed on a table: two strips of rubber cut from tires and reinforced with adhesive tape, for beating, and an electric cable with a plug at one end that can be placed directly into a socket, and at the other a clip to attach it to the finger, the foot, or the penis. Several of the wounded bear fresh marks of torture on their chest; one has a torso striped with blows, bright red, like raw meat. I take a copy of the videos. On them you can hear Abu Hamza's indignant voice as he tries to treat them with the nurse.

Abu Hamʒa left at the end of the interview, to go see his family in his home town. He was supposed to return two or three days later, and left me his phone number and his Skype ID, so I could contact him again. But in spite of repeated attempts I wasn't able to reach him for weeks or to get news of him, as is true for most of the people I met in Homs. On Monday, March 5, the British television network Channel 4 broadcast a report on his videos, claiming that they had been shot less than three months earlier, and not almost a year earlier as Abu Hamʒa had explained to me. Abu Hamʒa himself, filmed by Mani, appears in the report, his face blurred. Quite recently, I was finally able to reach him by Skype, in an Arab country where he was seeking material assistance for the opposition.

————

At 1:45 PM, as we're working on the computers, we're interrupted by another arrival and we go back downstairs. It's a ten-year-old boy and he is already dead, his chest pierced with a bullet that went through the heart. I stroke his thick, black hair; his complexion is already waxy. Gently, the doctor [*no longer Abu Hamʒa, who has left, but another one*] binds his hands with medical gauze. Standing at the door, his cousin, a mature man, looks at him weeping and repeating convulsively: "*Al-Hamdulillah, al-Hamdulillah, al-Hamdulillah.*" The medical staff lift the little boy, who is bare-chested, his head falls back, they carry him into an empty room next door where they lay him on the cold tiles, without a rug. An activist films the body, Ra'id photographs. Despite our presence he looks so alone. It's horribly pitiful.

His name was Taha B. He was killed in a car, and his sister was also wounded.

I turn to Ra'id. "When you're done, send a copy of your photo to the asshole from Gembloux, OK?"

After my departure, his father arrives. Overwhelmed, he calls to God: "Revenge on Bashar! May his children die like mine!" Another man explains to him that calling for vengeance against innocents goes against Islam. Ra'id tells me this later.

I go back upstairs to work and have a coffee. I've barely had a sip when another wounded man arrives, exactly thirty-five minutes after the boy, at 2:20 PM. A rather plump man, still conscious, with one shot that grazed his skull and another that got him in the chest, in the lower part of the lungs probably. He is surrounded by hysterical, ranting friends, whom I have to push forcibly out of the room so the doctors can work. One man in particular is sobbing convulsively and won't let go of the hand of his friend, who comments on his state: "My chest hurts. I'm having trouble breathing." They keep his head up, the doctor works with rapid gestures, the friends keep trying to force their way in and I have to push them back out again. Others crowd against the barred window shouting questions. The wounded man must have liquid in his lungs and they hastily evacuate him, in a mad throng, toward a taxi that shoots off, slams to an abrupt stop in front of the sniper street, backs up, starts again at a screech, crosses. Just afterwards, horrified, we see a few kids crossing at a run, then some young guys, an FSA soldier with his Kalashnikov. A bullet snaps just after him. Ra'id yells at Abu Brahim to forbid them from crossing. We go back in. The doctor tells us that the four people we've seen, the three wounded and the dead child, were hit by the same sniper from the post office. He gives the last wounded man a 20 percent chance of survival. We go back upstairs to work. My coffee is cold.

———

Arrival of a little group, an activist with two filmmakers from Damascus who are shooting a feature-length documentary on the revolution. I talk with one of them, O., who speaks good French and even better English.[49] He tells me about "*fringe groups*" around the FSA who commit crimes every day, kidnappings, murders of Alawite civilians. The FSA is disciplined and behaves well; but these little groups are made up of young men whose relatives have been killed or raped, and they believe they have the right. Which of course is giving in to the provocations of the regime. It's specific to Homs, it doesn't exist elsewhere. "There is a religious confrontation in Homs, that's undeniable. On both sides, there are serious discussions about ethnic cleansing."

"I'm a secular man from the cultural world. I must be here in this room. If I'm not, then it is a sectarian war. But if it develops better in other cities, then Homs will be

———

49 *Note to the Verso edition*: this was in fact 'Orwa Nyrabia, whom I have discussed at more length in the introduction. The second filmmaker, 'Orwa believes, was most likely Talal Derki, who directed *Return to Homs*. But his name does not figure in my notes.

contained. If a better version of the revolution prevails elsewhere, it will calm down the sectarianism here. The SNC is too slow for Homs, they are following the speed of the other cities, but Homs is going too fast.

"Homs is the worst place in Syria in terms of balanced clashes [*between the USA and the Army*]. But there are places far more devastated, Idlib for example."

O. continues: the FSA intervened in the entire urban belt around Damascus in a very well-coordinated and organized way. A carefully prepared offensive. The hierarchy down there is strict, and all the *katibas* answer directly to Riad al-Asa'ad in Antioch. Which is not the case for the *katibas* here, who are, as far as O. is concerned, another FSA, quasi-autonomous, like everything in Homs.

But there are positive developments, such as what the FSA in al-Khalidiya did in inviting 'Umar Shamsi to come train and lead them even though he isn't from the neighborhood.

———

4:45 PM. Another death, just next door. A man, killed by the same sniper, still the one from the post office. Abu Brahim goes to see if he can help the family. He already gave them money for the funeral, they didn't have enough.

News of the wounded. Two are still alive, but in serious condition. The first one did have internal bleeding but was operated on; as for the second one, they were able to place a drain in his lungs, but Security arrived at the hospital at that moment and he had to be evacuated at the last minute.

9:20 PM. Abu Brahim returns with the cellphone of the wounded man who was hit in the lungs, a Nokia shot right through. The bullet deviated toward the heart, but stopped one centimeter away, and the man was saved. The bullet to the head only grazed the bone.

————

11:00 PM. Abu Brahim returns to my question from dinner, about God and Evil. Theological discussion. My question: "How can God permit the death of a child like the one we saw today? Such an unjust death?" He asks for my point of view, which is that of an unbeliever, something disturbing for him: "*Mishkil.*"[50]

He quotes a proverb: "The traces show the path." The way the universe is put together shows there must indeed be a force that organizes it all. Then he follows with a parable: "There was a man who did not believe in God. He heard about a believer and wanted to talk with him. He liked to argue a lot, and always got the better in an argument. So he went to find the Muslim, a wise man. They agreed to meet at the Baghdad mosque, after the Friday prayer. Baghdad is crossed by the Tigris, you know. The unbeliever was waiting at the mosque and the Muslim was on the other side of the Tigris. So he was delayed. When he arrived, the unbeliever said to him, 'Why are you late?' – 'I was on the other side of the Tigris, and there was neither bridge nor boat. So I waited, until some floating pieces of wood gathered together to form a boat that carried me here.' – 'What, you want me to believe that the wood cut

———

50 "Problem."

itself on its own? Formed a boat on its own?' – 'And you? You want me to believe that this mosque, this city, this universe created themselves on their own?'"

And the question of Evil, then? "God has qualities." He names a certain number of them, including will. God has a will and the answer to my question is connected to that quality. God speaks, but without words and without speech. "From his will, he wanted to create good and evil. And he promoted good and forbade vice. He also wanted free will."

Objection from Ra'id: "But why want evil?" Volleys of Kalashnikov fire punctuate the conversation. The checkpoint is trying to scare people, and also to discourage the FSA from trying something. The conversation resumes but Abu Brahim always returns to the same arguments, which are in fact a profession of faith: "It's like that because it's like that." Hard for me to be satisfied with this, especially with a dead kid on the cold floor.

Monday, January 30
Al-Bayada – al-Khalidiya

Up early to call Ibn Pedro about my departure. We finally reach him around 9:30 AM. He is vague, evasive. "Yes, maybe, I might leave today, I don't know, I'll call you back."

A little later Marcel, the German journalist, calls me. He is stuck in Qusur, the *mukhabarat* and the Army are fighting on his street with the FSA, they're firing at his apartment. In Baba 'Amr, tank shelling.

The corpse of Taha, the boy from yesterday, has been transferred to the National Hospital. To recover him, the father has to sign papers certifying he was killed by a terrorist.

Two women completely in black come to see us. Their house was burned down and they want to testify. They live in the Sabil area. The older one chokes with emotion as she talks. Where they live, they are surrounded by Alawites on one side, Shiites on the other. Some men came around 2:00 AM, shot at the house, threw a grenade against the door, then a can of gas which they shot at, setting fire to the house. Half the house burned down before they managed to put out the fire. They didn't see the men but they were yelling: "We'll get you all out of here, you Sunnis!" Think they were Alawites supported by Security. Their neighbors' house was also attacked. There were seven Sunni families in the street, all have left except these two. It's been seventeen years that they've lived there. Abu Brahim goes to find them an apartment in the neighborhood.

Abu Bakr, Ra'id's activist friend, is here. He washed a dead man this morning and has come for a shower.

———

Noon. We have had several conversations on the phone with Marcel. He is still stuck, the shooting won't stop. A guy with him went out of the apartment and was killed. Nothing we can do. But Abu Brahim doesn't think Security will enter the buildings. Too afraid of FSA resistance.

We study our options. Ibn Pedro promises a departure tomorrow. I push for us to move to al-Khalidiya, to at least get past the obstacle of the snipers, now that they're relatively calm. Impossible to get from al-Khalidiya to Safsafi, clashes between the two sides in al-Warshat. But al-Khalidiya according to Abu Brahim is still accessible. He looks for an apartment for us with electricity and internet.

———

1:00 PM. Phone call from Abu Bilal. A second family massacred. It happened the same day as the other one, on

Thursday 26, but they weren't able to reach the bodies until today. They were brought to the Karam al-Zaytun clinic. There is the father, the mother, and four children, some of them with their throats slit. We move.

2:00 PM. Passage to al-Khalidiya without a problem. It's Abu 'Umar who brings us, in a Suzuki pickup. There's shooting in the streets we came by, so we take the back way, across the big "avenue of death." No shooting, on Cairo Street either, people are crossing on foot. On the way we pass just in front of a checkpoint, twenty meters away, but this one has agreed on a truce with the FSA.

We join Abu Bakr, who's going to stay with us. Wait in the street as Ra'id speaks to the BBC. The cool air feels good. My cough on the other hand has started up again, worse than ever.

We call Imad. Baba 'Amr is being shelled by twelve T-72s. The hospital is full, four dead, fifteen wounded. Yesterday there were eight tanks, the FSA destroyed four of them; the Army called in reinforcements, today the FSA destroyed another one. The bombing began the day before yesterday. All the dead in Baba 'Amr are civilians. Two killed by snipers, the rest by the bombing. The attack is toward Kfar 'Aaya, where the railroad runs. On the Jobar side it's calm. Imad says that someone who knows the way can pass. We'll see.

We call Hassan. He says twenty tanks since yesterday, and that they're completely powerless, they couldn't do anything against them.

Outside it just started up violently, after a lull, in Qusur probably. Marcel is still stuck.

———

Around 5:00 PM, I go out on foot with Abu Bakr, who is wearing a military jacket over a long imam's robe and who is looking more and more, with his red beard and his blazing eyes, like a Chechen fighter, and Najah, a young activist, to pick up Marcel who has finally managed to leave Qusur and is near the wooden clock-tower in Khalidiya. There are snipers and he is worried. We run across two streets, find one of his friends and then him; his friends bring us back in a car, a handsome black 4×4, fast and comfortable. Then I go to the internet café. Abu 'Adnan is there, surfing on his Samsung tablet. I show him the *Le Monde* pages online, he's rather pleased with them.

7:30 PM. Return to the house. News from the front: Abu Annas, the leader of the Friday demonstration in Bab Drib, was grievously wounded in the chest by a BTR shell. One of his friends was killed. Baba 'Amr is calmer.

Discussion with Marcel, who is going to stay with us, about the religious aspect of the uprising, on which he is focusing. He has met several shaykhs. Is trying to clarify the religious dynamics. It's very complicated, things are never stated clearly. Exchange of information and experiences.

Qusur is in fact a calm neighborhood. Marcel was out of luck. The *mukhabarat* mounted an operation to attack an FSA apartment, which they surrounded and pounded with

RPGs and machine guns. Two FSA soldiers were killed in the apartment, including Abu Amar Masarani, the FSA commander of Qusur. Five others fled and were shot at by snipers in the streets. Marcel, who wasn't far away, on the fourth floor of a neighboring building, tried to film from the balcony, but they were sniped at from a roof and his friend Muhammad was almost killed. Marcel was stuck for eight hours in the apartment, until the security forces withdrew.

Marcel talks about the Bedouins, who have a strong tradition of blood vengeance, who kidnap and kill in Alawite neighborhoods. "They're completely out of control," one guy told him, a revolutionary frightened by these excesses.

Abu Bakr tells us: three Bedouin women were kidnapped in Bayada (there are a lot of Bedouins in Bayada) by the *shabbiha*, a forty-year-old mother and her two daughters, aged sixteen and twelve. The three were raped, then returned after a month. Kept in an Alawite neighborhood, not in prison, near Sabil according to them. The family wanted to press charges, but that's of course impossible; and even if the state were functioning, the Bedouins would take revenge. So the relatives of the women kidnapped some men from the area where the women were prisoners, and demanded that their families hand over the rapists, under penalty of death for the captives. As the rapists weren't handed over, the captives were killed. "That's how the *fitna* began," concludes Abu Bakr. He adds that if that happened to him, he wouldn't take revenge like that. For him, the Qur'an forbids revenge on a third party. But the Bedouins are uncontrollable. Conflict too between them and the Shiites, and even the Iranians (because one of the girls said she heard Persian).

Marcel: when the Bedouins joined the FSA, they already had weapons for a long time; they're very active in combat, have had a lot of martyrs. They catch Army soldiers on leave and give them the choice: join the FSA or die.

He cites another case in al-Bayada which was a cause for vengeance: the first week of December, a Bedouin woman, seven months pregnant, leaned out of her door and caught a sniper bullet in the head. Her family avenged itself cruelly on the Alawites.

Marcel is convinced the regime wants a civil war, and is doing everything it can to provoke it.

Tuesday, January 31

Khalidiya – Baba 'Amr

Early awakening, breakfast then a crossing of the city in a sluggish taxi with fogged-up windows, in the company of Marcel who has decided to come with us. We pass just in front of a police checkpoint, government buildings with groups of officials in front, then the Safir Hotel. Stomach in knots but no problems. Baba 'Amr gray and empty. Return to Hassan's apartment where we wake up 'Alaa and Ahmad. They tell us about the fighting of the last few days: they destroyed two tanks yesterday, three the day before, wounded and killed some Army soldiers. No losses on their side. It is 9:30 AM, Ibn Pedro promises to come in an hour.

11:30 AM. Ibn Pedro still isn't here. Abu Yazan arrives. His friend wounded on Monday 23 is doing well, *al-Hamdulillah*. According to him, there are still ten tanks on the other side. Three have fled.

1:00 PM. Still no one. Time drags on. I read *The Life of Sylla* and wait, Mani works on his photos, and Marcel has left with the guys to the buildings at the front.

Ibn Pedro arrives soon after but ignores me rather royally. Marcel returns. Around 1:30 PM, shots and explosions, the guys waiting here grab their weapons and take off for the front to shoot back, Marcel and Ra'id at their heels.

Abu Yazan and a friend come to get hand grenades. Apparently there was shooting from snipers, one of the guys was wounded in the calf.

Comings and goings. A guy comes in to get an RPG, takes the launcher, but can't find the rockets. Abu Ja'far arrives with crates of provisions. Sporadic fire. Ibn Pedro has disappeared of course.

2:30 PM. The guys from the FSA counterattack and the firing is intense. We go out and run to Hassan's command post. Just as we arrive Ibn Pedro leaves at a run in the other direction, toward the apartment. With Ra'id we turn around to follow him. Brief exchange in the hallway as he gets ready to go out with a machine gun: "*Bukra sabah insha'Allah.*"[51] He seems unstable, furtive, ready to explode, we don't insist. Ra'id leaves with him for the CP and the area where the shooting continues. I'm exhausted and a little feverish, no courage to go play at war today, I remain alone in the apartment reading Plutarch, which is always better than wondering when I'll finally be able to get out of this fucking city.

3:30 PM. To the east, on the Kfar 'Aaya side, a building is burning, bombed by the Army apparently. Huge plume of black smoke through the gray sky above Baba 'Amr. The shooting resumes worse than ever.

_____

51   "Tomorrow morning, God willing."

The Cat explains: they have surrounded a building full of Army soldiers. There must be forty men in it, it's in the tower under construction next to the blue tower. The FSA is going to bring a loudspeaker to try to convince them to change sides. We'd like to go see, but they're firing mortars.

4:00 PM. We go out and run to the command post of Hassan, whom we find inside, sprawled on his sofa in a leather jacket and sneakers. The mortar shells are falling further away but they have received information from sympathizing Army officers that Grads[52] coming from Damascus are reaching the outskirts of Homs, with Baba 'Amr as their objective. We decide to withdraw to the center of the neighborhood. It is too late to go into town.

Imad arrives, along with two big pots full of carrots and stuffed zucchini, boiled, in sauce. Fadi comes by looking furious and glum: he just learned his cousin was killed yesterday. We wait for Imad to eat so we can leave. A little further on a muezzin keeps wailing *"Allahu Akbar"* in a particularly artificial, rasping voice. A little earlier on the other hand, when the sky cleared up briefly, a few rays of sun through the rain, the same loudspeaker was broadcasting very beautiful recitations of Qur'anic *suras*, punctuated by volleys of gunfire and explosions.

---

52   Multiple-rocket launcher system, mounted on a truck, with devastating firepower. They will in fact be deployed and start bombing Baba 'Amr on February 4.

We return to the apartment and I fall asleep pretty quickly, while the soldiers trickle back in. Just before that, a few mortar shells very close by. When I wake up, around 7:30 PM, Marcel is interviewing some soldiers with the help of Ra'id. I feel weak, feverish again. I insist that Ra'id have a serious conversation with Imad about the Ibn Pedro case. Ra'id finally explains to him that he thinks Ibn Pedro is jerking us around, and that he's behaving incorrectly toward us. Imad denies it, says there really are security problems. Slightly stormy argument, in which Hassan joins. Imad promises tomorrow, *insha'Allah*.

Around 8:00 PM, by lack of room, they send us to sleep in another apartment a little further away, in the basement but even closer to the front. Abu Yazan, who guides us there, confirms the information about the Grads, while insisting we're safe here. "The Army never enters the neighborhood at night." Marcel isn't very convinced. Discussion about what course to follow: sleep here or insist that they find us a pad nearer to the center of the neighborhood? Finally we stay.

Our new host is Lebanese, he comes from around Trablus,[53] but his mother is Syrian.

---

53   Tripoli.

Wednesday, February 1

Baba 'Amr

Slept well despite the cold. Dreams: riots, automatic weapons, beach, students, episodes combining these elements. When I wake up, around 9:00 AM, a few mortar shells, a little further away. Our host has left but one of his friends makes us breakfast.

We go out to phone, the apartment doesn't have any reception. In front of Hassan's command post, 'Alaa, Fadi, and some other guys are drinking tea, beneath a newly installed awning to keep out the rain. It's nice out. Ra'id calls Ibn Pedro: he has guests, and no planned time for departure. He'll call back. Abu Bilal informs him about the situation at the center: there is fighting everywhere, Safsafi is cut off, it's really war.

'Alaa explains their plans for the soldiers surrounded in the building: they're going to mine the supporting pillars, then give them a choice between coming over to their side, or being blown up.

The mortars start up again, one very close, Ra'id hears it whistle. I tell him it's good if you can hear the whistle: if you can hear the whistle, it's not for you. He looks rather unconvinced.

11:30 AM. It's raining now. Still no news from Ibn Pedro. We go to the mosque, where I remain sitting in a corner, alone, as Ra'id goes out to attend to his affairs. Little by little, the men come in to pray.

We go to the school [*the headquarters of the Military Council*]. Muhannad isn't there. There's an Irish woman journalist, with Jeddi and Danny, looking harassed. Jeddi yells at Ra'id: "Danny, translate. I'm fed up with him! He wants war, war, war. Humanitarian questions don't interest him." Ra'id: "No need to translate, my friend." The young woman wants to leave tomorrow, and I ask to leave with her, in case.

I had met Danny Abdul Dayem, a young twenty-three-year-old Syrian-Brit, at Abu Bari's clinic the same day we arrived in Homs, and I was struck by his perfect English, a very rare thing here. He himself was just returning from vacation in England, and welcomed my suggestion to come work with me. During the following days it was impossible for me to find him or even to speak with him on the phone. We would learn later on that he had immediately been picked up by the Information Bureau, with whom we didn't have the best relations. After my departure, when the systematic bombing of Baba 'Amr began, Danny began appearing several times a day on YouTube, denouncing in English the atrocities filmed by the activists and calling for international help. On February 13, as the shelling was intensifying, he left Baba 'Amr to find refuge in Lebanon. He has since then granted several interviews to English-language television networks about the horrors he witnessed.

1:00 PM. We find Imad in front of Hassan's command post, looking harassed, I don't know if it's because of us or some-thing else. No sign of Ibn Pedro. "The way isn't free," Imad states, tired. I return to the apartment, at least it's warm.

A feeling of imprisonment takes shape. It's been five days now that I've been trying to leave, the guys are furtive, not clear, there's shelling, Ra'id is annoyed by everything, me, the situation, his computer that keeps crashing, the phone network doesn't work well and it's hard to communicate, it's what is called a shitty situation, I guess. And there is absolutely nothing to be done.

Visit to Imad's clinic, to look for Abu Salim. He isn't there. In front of the clinic, stickers from the Syrian Arab Red Crescent, laughable protection. Work setting up the oper-ating room. Quick visit from 'Abd ar-Razzaq Tlass, who has come to see how the work is advancing. Several wounded: a person badly burned, after a gas explosion caused by a mortar shell on Monday, a man machine-gunned Sunday at a checkpoint in Insha'at, a young guy with his face burned who caught the backfire of a shell that fell at the foot of his building, through the window of his apartment, five days ago. Now he's doing better, he explains all this to us with his face covered with cream, and shows us a photo of himself taken a few days ago, his head completely wrapped in bandages. The man wounded by bullets is a taxi driver who was coming from Damascus with a passenger and who was machine-gunned at 4:00 AM by a checkpoint.

Arrival of Dr. 'Ali, the living martyr. "Yesterday was a slaughter." Seventeen wounded. Of course, no one told us anything, or showed us anything.

Around 4:00 PM, arrival of Abu Hanin, from the Information Bureau, the Maktab al-I'ilami. He immediately tears into me, in English. "I don't even know you," I reply. "Yes, but I spoke with him last week," he says, pointing to Ra'id. "He said he'd be back in ten minutes, and you guys disappeared." The Irish woman is leaving in half an hour. Can't I go with her? "No, you can't. You guys say you are on your own, fine, you say you can manage, fine, now manage with your people." Things are getting out of hand. Ra'id intervenes and it starts, half in English, half in Arabic.

Abu Hanin: "You see, we are Arabs. This is how it is with Arabs." Ra'id: "This has nothing to do with Arabs. I'm Arab too." The guy is grotesque, aggressive, incoherent. We sense he can't stand the fact that we bypassed them. Finally, he turns to me: "Why do you say to him you cannot go because we have a problem? I never said that. You have fresh material, of course it is in our interest that you publish it. If we can help you go out, we will. But we can't. You can't go with the woman." I try to smooth things out, finally he gives me a sensible explanation: "She's leaving in a truck, veiled, disguised as a Syrian woman, with Syrian papers. You think you can leave like that? You think so?" I do my best to calm him down, smooth over the misunderstanding, but he is out of control. Finally, we agree that he'll help me if he can.

In the apartment. Tea, reading. A few men are sleeping or resting. Around 5:30 PM, a series of mortar shells, not far, near the cemetery. Hassan arrives with his two boys, very cute and shy. The guys have the children play with pistols, safety on but loaded.

6:00 PM. An Mi-24 combat helicopter is whirling around the neighborhood. The guys are unhappy with the performance of Alain Juppé at the Security Council. They start playing a video game, soccer. Ra'id disappeared hours ago, no news.

I ask 'Alaa to take me on motorbike to find Ra'id. He doesn't know where to go but we'll look. We weave through the puddles, go down a long avenue with our lights out, reach the second health center, Imad's, then from there the clinic, the one where we were this afternoon; there, they direct us to a first activists' house, but it's the one where we had met the Communist lawyer, there are just a few guys there, finally we find the apartment of the *maktab*. Ra'id is indeed here, with Marcel, working on his computer to try to save his files. I thank 'Alaa who leaves.

There are dozens of activists sprawled everywhere, glued to their laptops, all on YouTube or Facebook or Twitter. Someone offers me a chicken and fries sandwich and lends me a Mac, e-mail finally, terribly slow. The Irish journalist has already left. Abu Hanin probes me: "Why didn't you come see us? Why did you avoid us?" I answer diplomatically. When I mention the term *al-Maktab al-I'ilami*, Abu Hanin denies that such a bureau exists: "We're just a group of friends, that's all." On the walls, photos of martyrs. Brief political discussion, but it doesn't go far.

More discussions later. Abu Hanin tells me that if our guys can get me across the *autostrad*, his can take care of the rest. Promises me that if there is a way, he'll get me out tomorrow or Saturday. Friday isn't good, it's a dangerous day because of the demonstrations.

Ra'id is completely absorbed in his computer problems and barely pays attention when I talk to him. Finally I leave him there and have a friend of the living martyr take me back to the apartment.

Thursday, February 2

Baba 'Amr – al-Qusayr – border – Beirut

10:30 AM. Breakfast of bread, olive oil, *ʒaʿatar*, green olives, and tea with Hassan, Imad, and Ahmad. No sign of Ra'id. Imad assures me I'm leaving today, communicates that Ibn Pedro is checking out the route. No one answers the phone. We wait.

11:00 AM. Ra'id arrives. Vague, evasive, exhausted after having spent the night on his computer, barely says hello. Speaks with Imad but doesn't translate anything, doesn't explain anything. Then goes to the neighbor's place where we had slept the day before yesterday. Five minutes later, arrival of Ibn Pedro. "*Yallah.*" I want to wait for Ra'id, but he refuses: "*Yallah, yallah.*" I get into a car where there are already two other people who are also leaving. Departure. I call Paris and explain the situation, but no way to reach Ra'id, who still hasn't changed his SIM card.

Two phone networks function in Homs, Syriatel and MTN. Ra'id had an MTN number but, since our return to Baba 'Amr, MTN was working more and more poorly; Syriatel too, actually, but better than MTN. I had thus suggested to Ra'id that he switch to Syriatel, which he would do a little later on. A few days later, all the cellphone networks in Homs were cut off. As I write this, they still haven't been re-established.

Crossing of the *autostrad*. It is 12:40 PM. In a house a little further on, the men who left in front of us are praying while they wait for us. Despite his difficult, temperamental side, Ibn Pedro has a magnificent illuminated smile, which lights up as soon as prayer is over.

We separate: the other two leave one way, me the other, with Ibn Pedro and a driver, in a little Suzuki pickup truck, directly for Lebanon apparently. Ibn Pedro has a Kalashnikov stuck between his legs, the driver is armed too, if we come across a flying checkpoint things will go sour. On the road, the two men remain glued to their cellphones, Ibn Pedro has three, the network doesn't work well at all but from time to time they receive information. The sun is shining, it illuminates all the flat countryside and the murky puddles, we alternate between muddy paths and well-traveled roads, passing through several villages; in the distance, the Djebel Lubnan bars the horizon, pale blue, a long fringe of white clouds clinging to its snowy peaks. It's warm in the passenger compartment, the truck jolts along, we pass smugglers on motorbikes loaded with jerrycans of fuel oil, farmers on tractors, Bedouin camps, green, muddy fields.

1:30 PM. Stop in a village. On the TV, Isma'il Haniyeh. The driver who dropped off the other two joins us, it's Abu

'Abdallah, the same man who had brought us to Homs. No idea of the waiting time, no one tells me anything and in any case I'd be hard pressed to understand. I try to resume the *Comparison of Lysander with Sylla*, but they bring me lunch, copious and superb as usual, with hard-boiled eggs and *ful* in sauce. Afterwards, I read, the wait stretches on. Ra'id finally calls and confirms that they're taking me directly to Lebanon, *insha'Allah*.

2:30 PM. We leave, with Abu 'Abdallah. Roads, villages, then a muddy, rutted path, the same one we took going in. We pass endless streams of trucks and vans, transporting merchandise in the other direction. Then again a road where we meet up, to my immense pleasure, with my old friend Fury and his aging pickup. He takes me with Ibn Pedro to al-Qusayr, to the same house we had stayed at on the way in, Abu Amar's, who is still as welcoming and warm. Mayte [*Carrasco, a Spanish journalist friend, who works for TV Cinco*] is in town, Fury takes me to where she's staying with her colleagues, and I quickly explain the situation to them. They've been in al-Qusayr for five days, they're still waiting to get into the city. Could Ibn Pedro bring them in? I go back to Abu Amar's house with the activist who's shepherding them, a guy from al-Qusayr who speaks a little English. Ibn Pedro's answer: I'll take them if Abu Hanin asks me to. But Abu Hanin can't be reached. *Bukra sabah, insha'Allah.*

Fury receives a phone call: the way is clear. At 4:30 PM we leave, again piled into the pickup's cabin, three of us with Ibn Pedro. The Kalashnikov is still there, but first we go to

drop it off at the farm where we had gone to meet the commander, on the way in; Fury, however, keeps his grenade,
which he waves in front of me, laughing. We also stop by
another house from which he emerges with a small bag full
of dollars, 100-dollar bills, the famous "Ben Franklins,"
and wads of Syrian pounds, as well as a box of dates, soft
and exquisite. The journey to the border takes an hour, the
same roads as we took on the way in. The sun sets behind
the Jabal, the puddles shine in the mud like pale yellow mir-
rors, the sky turns pale, everything is blue and brown and
green. Traffic jams of trucks of all sizes at an FSA checkpoint, the vans get stuck in the mud, the men push. Fury
and Ibn Pedro have a discussion, I don't know about what.
Then finally a road, Fury pushes his pickup to 100–120
kph, it's even more terrifying than the possibility of a flying
checkpoint. Detour to drop by a house where thick wads of
Syrian pounds are stacked next to the *sobia*. "*Bukra Lubnan*,"
the host, an obese man, tells me with a big smile, "*alyoum
hun*." Me, crestfallen: "What, *fi mishkil? Alyoum maf fi
Lubnan?*"[54] Fury laughs: "*Yallah, yallah*." In fact the man
just wanted to offer me hospitality, as is the custom.
Fortunately they're no Georgians, he doesn't insist. As we
leave, in the cabin, Ibn Pedro stuffs the wads of bills into a
plastic bag, the same wads that were near the *sobia* I think.
Fury barrels down the roads, night falls, he passes other
vehicles without slowing down, speeds through a village,
weaving between motorbikes and pedestrians in the dark.
Finally, in another village, a house, the same one as on the

---

54   "Lebanon, tomorrow. Today you stay here." – "There's a problem?
We're not going to Lebanon today?" – "Let's go, let's go."

way in, with the same host. Brief wait, the motorbikes are coming to get us. With night the cold has come, I'm freezing on the motorbike that bumps between the puddles with its lights out, the driver guides himself from the light of the moon. Above the stars are shining, I recognize Orion, the Pleiades. Crossing.[55] Some young soldiers are warming themselves and joking in a hut, the motorbike stalls, no problem. Another house: outside, in front of a brazier, I warm my hands, alone for a moment, it's wonderfully soothing.

After they usher me into the reception room of the house. There's an old gentleman with a baby on his knees, to whom I give some cough drops, and, a rare thing, a lady who starts invoking Allah when I tell her I have two children. Then it's time to leave. Ibn Pedro has disappeared, and Fury, with whom I take a souvenir photo, isn't coming. We say our farewells and Fury packs me into a small pickup truck loaded with God knows what, together with two farmers, a skinny little guy with a moustache and a fat one, repeating "Beirut, Beirut" with a big smile. *Davai*, Beirut, apparently from here on it's easy. In fact it's going to be the Keystone Cops, probably the worst part of the journey. A kilometer further on, they motion to me to get out of the vehicle, together with the fat gut: we're approaching a Lebanese Army checkpoint, we have to go around it. The fat guy takes my bag and we begin walking through plowed

55   *Note to the Verso Edition*: See note 7, p. 29, as to why the passage of the last Syrian Army checkpoint before the border could not be described in the original edition.

fields, the mud is sticky but fortunately not too soft. Very soon, I realize that we're walking right through the white light of the checkpoint's spotlight, my shadow stretches across the plowed field for a dozen meters, they must see us as in broad daylight and it would be a pigeon shoot. They don't shoot, we slowly emerge from the spotlight's beam, but the fat guy starts running, I follow as well as I can, we cover maybe half a kilometer like that, dogs are barking around the checkpoint, in the distance I can see the pickup, which on its side has passed the checkpoint, stopped with all its lights off. Just at that instant a vehicle arrives on the road, we run and I jump into the pickup with the fat guy, just in time. It's a civilian truck, if it had been an Army vehicle we'd have been fucked.

We start off, rejoin the highway where we had met the motorbikes on the way in, and we speed up, going as fast as the old heap allows, which isn't bad. Then finally we arrive in front of a big checkpoint, the border post apparently. The guys park right next to it, alongside another pickup truck, and we get out. There's a dubious-looking shop in front of the checkpoint, to the right, with an impassive man in a *keffiyeh* standing in front. I follow the mustachioed farmer inside and watch him exchange a few words with the storekeeper. Then I go back out, still under the gaze of the man in the *keffiyeh*. The fat guy grabs me, drags me next to the shop, and motions to me to pretend to piss. I pretend to piss. When he turns around, I turn around too. Just in front of the checkpoint, a massive man with a crew cut and a leather jacket, who's just getting out of a military-looking jeep, starts yelling at me in Arabic. He's obviously an officer, even if he isn't in uniform. I look at him, shrug my shoulders, and head for the pickup truck. Next to me, the fat guy smiles at him inanely. We get into the pickup and start up. The officer has already lost interest in us and is heading for the shop. We make a U-turn and start at top speed on the main road. I look, but the military isn't following us. Out of precaution, I erase the souvenir photos of Fury. After a few kilometers, finally, we turn on to a dirt path to the right of the road. I wonder why the hell we just didn't take it straight off. Jolts, we skirt round the checkpoint, enter the town from above, in front of a big modern church, then we find the road again and continue on. A little further on we pass another checkpoint, but it's a normal Army checkpoint, we pass without trouble.

Further on, the two farmers stop a minivan and bundle me into it: "Taxi, taxi, Beirut." Long journey via Ba'albik, passengers get in and out. In Chtaura, before the climb, a young woman gets in and sits in front: the first woman's hair I've seen for eighteen days, aside from Mayte's. During the ascent, stop at a supermarket, the driver's assistant and one of his pals buy some wine and offer me some in a plastic cup: coarse, rough, bad, it's divine. The pass is snow-covered and very beautiful in the night. Then it's the long descent toward Beirut.

Rip-off attempt at arrival, when I get dropped off at a traffic circle, they want $100, I get away with $50, fuck it. Taxi, an old gentleman who speaks English with a West African accent and who has lived in Liberia for thirty years, he knew the late Samuel Doe – "He was just a lieutenant, not even a captain, he was a nice guy. Yes, he died really bad. They dragged him all through town" – and Charles Taylor, who still owes him $50. Incredulous, I burst out laughing: "Charlie Taylor owes you fifty dollars?" He laughs when I suggest he write to The Hague to demand the money. He drops me off at Le Rouge, in Hamra. Jameson and cigarillo at the bar as I wait for L. My boots are still covered in mud from the roads and the fields, I haven't changed since Sunday and I stand out like a sore thumb in this chic restaurant, it's totally surreal after the breakfast in Baba 'Amr with Hassan, Imad, and Ahmad. I catch the Air France flight at 2:00 AM, straight after the meal, without even taking a shower, and finish writing these notes as I wait for takeoff. Already, for hours now, all this is turning into a story.

Epilogue

It's only after I wrote all this, and left Syria, that things in Homs really went haywire. I thought that what I had seen was violent enough, and I thought I knew what violent means. But I was wrong. For the worst was only just beginning, which makes me ashamed, today, as I reread them, of certain passages, the ones for instance where I report our idiotic quarrels with the Baba 'Amr activists, quarrels that took place and had their meaning (which is why I'm not censoring those passages), but that take on a whole different meaning in light of what would follow, and the ulterior behavior of the interested parties, Jeddi and Abu Hanin to name just two, to whom several Western journalists owe their lives.

In brief: on the night of February 3, the day after my departure, several shells fell on the neighborhood of Khalidiya, very close to the Square of Free Men. They were spaced out, and all struck more or less in the same place, which cannot be a coincidence. Consequently, the people who rushed to help the victims of the first shells (including, I've already noted, Maẓhar Tayara, aka 'Umar the Syrian) were killed or grievously wounded in turn. Telephones were still working and I called

Mani, who was still in Baba 'Amr. I would have liked to know the fate of quite a few people – Abu 'Adnan, Abu Bakr, Najah (they survived, that episode at least), the barber in the square, Abu Yassir the baker, the mechanic and his friends, the two kebab vendors – but I just asked him to find out about one person: Mahmoud, the little ten-year-old boy who, during the demonstrations, danced and chanted slogans on the shoulders of the grown-ups. Mani was never able to tell me anything about him. By then many other people were already dead. On Saturday the 4th, the Army intensified its shelling of Baba 'Amr, and on the 6th or the 7th, I'm not quite sure, the telephone network was cut off for good. Mani was at that time in the center of the city and, along with the editorial board of Le Monde, *we somewhat lost track of him, until he emerged from Homs in turn on February 11. As for my friend Mayte Carrasco, she had entered Baba 'Amr with her two colleagues, and she lived through several days of bombings before coming back out with them as well as Paul Wood from the BBC, through the famous tunnel which was much talked about later on, but which at that time was still the secret of secrets (I should point out, since my text remains deliberately vague about this, that I myself never left through the tunnel), and then spending another three weeks in al-Qusayr.*

Almost all the contact we could have with the activists were cut off at that point, except with the two groups that had a BGAN satellite system, the activists in al-Khalidiya and in Baba 'Amr. I thus lost all trace of Abu Brahim, the shaykh from al-Bayada, and of doctor Abu Hamza who worked with him, as well as of the Safsafi activists 'Umar Talawi, Abu Bilal, and the others. After Mani came out, we no longer had any more news of the al-Khalidiya activists. I was able to have sporadic contacts through Skype, usually by chat, with Abu Hanin and another Baba 'Amr activist who changes his pseudonym so often I can no longer be sure who he is (he's one of the young men we met at the home of Dr. 'Ali on the evening of January 22, but I'm not sure which one). Every day, on YouTube, videos appeared, each one more disgusting than the last, commented on, until his evacuation to Lebanon, by the Syro-Brit Danny Dayem, then very often by a young doctor — or rather probably a medical student, I'm not sure — whom I had met several times but who doesn't appear in these notebooks, Dr. Muhammad al-Muhammad. One thing was obvious, the pounding of the neighborhood was intensifying every day (we didn't know much about the other neighborhoods, but it didn't seem any better), and the number of civilian victims kept increasing. Those of you who don't have too much trouble sleeping should take the time to watch some of these videos, I invite you to.

Baba 'Amr has a peculiarity, which I had noticed but at the time hadn't taken the full measure of: it had been built in haste and semi-legally, by people of little means rejected on the fringes of Homs, and thus to whom the digging of a basement, during the construction of their little building, seemed superfluous. A basement can be very useful, to put away old furniture or store potatoes and onions, but you can do without it when you never throw away your furniture and when your store of potatoes and onions can fit easily in the kitchen. It's quite a different thing when a modern army, equipped with assault tanks, Grad rockets, and mortars of various calibers all the way up to 240 mm — a weapon never deployed in a contemporary conflict, aside from Chechnya — pounds your neighborhood street by street, house by house, in an orderly, systematic way, for twenty-seven full days. I'll quote here the British photographer Paul Conroy, who miraculously survived (thanks to the help of the activists of Baba 'Amr) the last of those days: "They've living in bombed-out wrecks, children six to a bed, rooms full of people waiting to die." And many did die, while elsewhere people were talking.

For indeed, people were seriously talking. The offensive of Bashar al-Assad's forces had begun, in an interesting coincidence, the day after a vote by the UN Security Council on a rather weak resolution, based on the Arab League's peace plan, but nonetheless firmly vetoed by Russia and China. Little eager to repeat their Libyan adventure, even when it turned out that the massacre, so much feared in Benghazi, was actually underway in Homs, American and European diplomats were bogging themselves down in rather ridiculous discussions about "humanitarian corridors" or some such propositions. Their Arab colleagues, Qatari or Saudi, were beginning to murmur that a more forceful intervention might be imaginable, notably through weapon deliveries to the FSA, but no one was listening to them. It was at this point, running out of patience, that I suggested in the last of my articles in Le Monde *that we shut up and abandon the Syrians to their fate. Alas, that's just what we did.*

The epic of Western journalists killed or wounded in Baba 'Amr directed the spotlight on what was happening there, and at the same time paradoxically diverted attention from it. On the one hand, no one could say any longer that they didn't know exactly what was going on there; on the other, they could fill the TV reports and newspaper columns with (more than deserved) homages to Marie Colvin and Rémi Ochlik — killed

on February 22 in a rocket bombardment targeting the house of
the "information bureau" — then concentrate all the attention of
diplomacy and media on the saving of the journalists wounded
in that same attack, Édith Bouvier and Paul Conroy, as well as
two others who had chosen to stay with them rather than evacuate through the tunnel, Javier Espinosa and William Daniels.
I have no words to describe their courage, or the nightmare they
lived through until they managed one after another to reach
Lebanon, a week later. But I will also note that, with a few rare
exceptions, none of the Western media mentioned the Syrian
activists and journalists who were with them, except at the end,
when thirteen unidentified "militants" were killed during the
catastrophic exfiltration of the wounded.

After leaving Homs, the journalists themselves did not fail
to pay homage to those who had helped them, or to speak with
very precise and harsh words of the carnage taking place to
almost general indifference. Yes, some of our leaders have
forcefully condemned it; still, they let it continue. People will
say to me they had no choice. I would answer that you always
have a choice, as did those who in Syria rose up against Bashar
al-Assad and his putrid, senile, and ultimately doomed regime.

I have little news of the Syrians who became, in a few days, our
friends. It seems that most of the information activists and the
medical staff in Baba 'Amr (including Abu Hanin and
Muhammad al-Muhammad) were able to evacuate with the
surviving FSA just before the definitive fall of the neighborhood, on Friday, March 2, except for Jeddi, who chose to
remain; on April 1, Jeddi, whose real name is 'Ali 'Uthman,
was arrested in Aleppo, and has apparently since then been subjected to severe torture. The activists in Safsafi, al-Khalidiya,

and al-Bayada — 'Umar Talawi, Abu Bilal, Abu 'Adnan, Abu Bakr, and Abu Brahim — are, according to Mani's sporadic information, still alive, even though their situation remains very difficult. Fadi, 'Alaa, Abu Yazan, Ahmad, and all the other FSA fighters who appear in these notebooks must be dead or worse — or maybe not, but I'll probably never know. Of many of those I've named here, by their first name, an initial, or the name they chose for themselves when they threw themselves into this adventure, there will probably remain nothing beyond these notes, and their memory in the minds of those who knew and loved them: all those young guys in Homs, smiling and full of life and courage, for whom death, or an atrocious wound, or ruin, failure, and torture were nothing compared to the incredible joy of having cast off the dead weight crushing, for forty years, the shoulders of their fathers.

Paris, April 11, 2012.

Table of Ranks

Arabic	Transliteration	English
مشير	Mushir	Marshal
فريق أول	Fariq Awwal	Lieutenant General
فريق	Fariq	Major General
عماد أول	Imad Awwal	1st Imad
عماد	Imad	Imad
لواء عميد	Liwa Amid	Brigadier General
عقيد	Aqid	Colonel
مقدم	Muqaddam	Lieutenant-Colonel
رائد	Ra'id	Major
نقيب	Naqib	Captain
ملازم أول	Mulazim Awwal	Lieutenant
ملازم	Mulazim	Second Lieutenant
رقيب	Raqib	Sergeant
عريف	Arif	Corporal

Source: Human Rights Watch